1144 Random, Interesting & Fun Facts You Need To Know

The Knowledge Encyclopedia To Win Trivia

Scott Matthews

The more that you read, the more things you will know. The more you learn, the more places you'll go.

- Dr. Seuss

7 BENEFITS OF READING FACTS

1. Knowledge
2. Stress Reduction
3. Mental Stimulation
4. Better Writing Skills
5. Vocabulary Expansion
6. Memory Improvement
7. Stronger Analytical Thinking Skills

ABOUT THE AUTHOR

Scott Matthews is a geologist, world traveller and author of the "Amazing World Facts" series! He was born in Brooklyn, New York, by immigrant parents from Ukraine but grew up in North Carolina. Scott studied at Duke University where he graduated with a degree in Geology and History.

His studies allowed him to travel the globe where he saw and learned amazing trivial knowledge with his many encounters. With the vast amount of interesting information he accumulated, he created his best selling books "Random, Interesting & Fun Facts You Need To Know."

He hopes this book will provide you with hours of fun, knowledge, entertainment and laughter.

If you gain any knowledge from this book, think it's fun and could put a smile on someone's face, he would greatly appreciate your review on Amazon. You can scan the QR code below which will take you straight to the review page!

Table of Contents

Airplanes & Airports

1.　Turbulence on an airplane cannot be predicted. It can occur even on a cloudless, clear day.

2.　Airports had to standardize their names in the 1930's with airport codes, so those with two letter names simply added an "x", hence names such as LAX.

3.　During an emergency landing, a plane has the ability to dump its fuel from the wings to prevent it from exploding if it crashes.

4.　You're not allowed to take mercury onto a commercial passenger plane as it can damage the aluminum the plane is made out of.

5.　The first commercial flight only lasted twenty three minutes and cost $8,500 in today's money. It was between St. Petersburg, Florida, and Tampa, Florida.

6.　It's possible to see a rainbow as a complete circle from an airplane.

7.　The filtration technology used in airplanes is the same technology they use to filter air in hospitals.

8.　The rules of most airlines require that the pilot and co-pilot of a plane eat different meals. This is just in case one of the meals causes food poisoning.

9.　For less than the cost of a Ferrari you can buy a renovated Boeing 737.

10.　The average Boeing 747 plane has 160 miles (260 kilometers) of wiring inside of it.

11.　The Antonov An-225 is the largest aircraft ever made and was initially created for the task of transporting spaceplanes. It weighs 285 tons, has a wingspan of 288 feet (eighty-eight meters), and cost $250 million.

12.   In 2014, a man in China bought a first class ticket on China Eastern Airlines, went to the airport, and ate free food for almost an entire year in the VIP lounge. Astoundingly, he cancelled and re-booked his flight an incredible 300 times over the course of the year and then cancelled his ticket for a full refund once the airline became wise of his scam.

13.   Most airplane crashes happen either three minutes after taking off or eight minutes before landing.

14.   MI-5 once planned to use gerbils to detect terrorists and spies at airports, given that their great sense of smell could acutely detect increased adrenaline in people. However, the project was abandoned when they noticed that the gerbils were not able to tell the difference between terrorists and those who were just afraid of flying.

Amazing

15. In 1993, a Chinese man named Hu Songwen was diagnosed with kidney failure. In 1999, after no longer being able to afford the hospital bills, he built his own dialysis machine which kept him alive for another thirteen years.

16. The longest possible uninterrupted train ride in the world is over 10,000 miles (17,000 kilometers) long which goes from Vietnam to Portugal.

17. The Solvay Hut is the world's most dangerously placed mountain hut, located 13,000 feet (3,962 meters) above ground level in Switzerland.

18. At the 1912 Olympics, a Japanese marathon runner named Shizo Kanakuri quit and went home without telling officials and he was considered a missing person in Sweden for fifty years. In 1966, he was invited to complete the marathon, finishing with a total time of fifty four years, eight months, six days, and five hours.

19. Carmen Dell'Orefice is the world's oldest working model. She started modelling at the age of fifteen and is still an active model to this day at the age of eighty three.

20. In 2005, a Nepalese couple climbed Everest and got married on its peak.

21. In 1955, a six hundred year old plaster Buddhist statue was dropped when it was being moved locations only to reveal that the plaster was covering another Buddhist statue made of solid gold inside.

22. In 2011, archaeologists discovered the skeletal remains of a Roman couple who had been holding hands for over 1,500 years.

23. The Shangri-La Hotel in China captured a record for the largest ball pit ever created

measuring eighty two by forty one feet (twenty five by thirteen meters) and contained over a million balls.

24. The average led pencil can draw a line that will be thirty five miles (fifty six kilometers) long.

25. Keikyu Aburatsubo Marine Park is an aquarium located in Japan where you can shake hands with otters.

26. In 2011, archaeologists at the ground zero 9/11 terrorist attack site in New York City uncovered half of an 18th century ship; it's believed to have once been used by merchants.

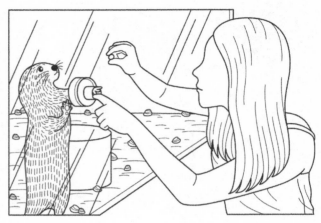

27. In Finland, there is a giant rock named Kummakivi that is sitting perfectly on a seemingly curved mound. The name translates to "strange rock" since nobody knows how it got there.

28. When Jadav Payeng was sixteen, he began planting trees since he was concerned for the disappearing habit for the local animals. He continued doing this for over thirty five years. Today he has single handedly restored more than 1,360 acres of forest.

29. The youngest person to ever climb Everest was young Jordan Romero at the age of thirteen.

30. Philani Dladla is a homeless man from Johannesburg, South Africa, who's known as the pavement bookworm. He survives by reviewing books for people passing on the street and sells them the book if they like it.

31. The human brain cell, the universe, and the Internet all have similar structures.

32. Jose Mujica, a former president of Uruguay, was the poorest president in the world at the time as he gave away most of his income to charity.

33. Stephen Hawking was diagnosed with ALS at twenty one and was expected to die at twenty five. He lived till seventy.

34. The oldest living person on earth, whose age has been verified, is Japanese Misao Okawa, who is 116 years old.

35. The most powerful organism is the Gonorrhea bacteria which can pull up to 100,000 times their size.

36. Sixty three year old former math professor Joan Ginther, who has a PhD in statistics from Stanford University, has won the scratch and lottery four separate times for a grand total of $20.4 million. She never revealed how she did it, but the odds of accomplishing what she did is one in eighteen septillion.

37. A Californian couple named Helen and Les Brown were both born on December 31,

1918, were married for seventy five years, and then died one day apart at the age of ninety four in 2013.

38. A woman from Michigan named Barbara Soper gave birth on 8/8/8, 9/9/9, and 10/10/10, the odds of which are fifty million to one.

39. In 1860, Valentine Tapley, a pike County farmer and loyal democrat, promised to never trim his beard again if Abraham Lincoln was elected president. He kept his word and his beard grew to 12.5 feet (3.8 meters) long.

40. If we somehow discovered a way to extract gold from the core of Earth, we would be able to cover all the land in gold up to our knees.

41. When he was a freshman in 1987, a man named Mike Hayes got a friend, who worked at the Chicago Tribune, to write him an article asking the millions who read it to donate one penny each towards his tuition. Immediately, pennies, nickels, and even larger donations came pouring in from all over the world. After accumulating the equivalent of 2.9 million pennies, he graduated and paid for his degree in Food Science.

42. There is a metal called "gallium" that melts in your hand.

43. In 2010, a black Nigerian couple living in the UK gave birth to a blond white baby with blue eyes that they called "the miracle baby."

44. In the 1980's, a man known only as George, who had severe OCD, shot himself in the head in an attempt to commit suicide. Instead of the bullet killing him, it destroyed the part of the brain that was causing the OCD and he went on to get straight A's in college five years later.

45. Real diamonds don't show up in x-rays.

46. Adam Rainer, an Australian man, is the only person in medical history to have been classified as both a dwarf and a giant in his lifetime. He stood at 3.8 feet (1.17 meters) on his twenty first birthday and he was classified as a dwarf; but by the time he died at the age of fifty one, he stood at seven feet and six inches (2.34 meters) tall due to a growth spurt.

47. In 1983, a sixty one year old potato farmer named Cliff Young, who was not an athlete, won the 544 mile (875 kilometer) Sydney to Melbourne Ultra Marathon. This was simply because he ran while the other runners slept.

48. By the time Donald Trump was twenty seven, he owned 14,000 apartments.

49. In the 1960's, the US did an experiment where two people without nuclear training

had to design a nuke with only access to publicly available documents. They succeeded.

50.   Stamatis Moraitis was diagnosed by doctors with cancer and was told he only had a couple of months to live. He was still alive ten years later and went back to tell the doctors that he was still alive only to find out that the doctors who diagnosed him had passed away. Stamatis lived until he was one hundred and two.

51.   In 2013, a man named Harrison Okene survived for three days at the bottom of the ocean in a sunken ship by finding a pocket of air.

52.   Over a hundred people drew for the second prize of the Powerball Lotto in 2005. It was suspected that cheating was going on, however, later it was discovered that the winners had simply used the same numbers they'd received in a fortune cookie.

53.   There are more than 150 people cryofrozen right now in the hopes that one day the technology will be invented to revive them, with over 1,000 people registered to do the same upon their death.

54.   In 1978, a US Navy ship known as the USS Stein was found to have traces of an unknown species of giant squid attack. Almost all cuts on the sonar dome contained remains of a sharp, curved claw that were found on the rims of the suction cups of some squid tentacles, but some of the claw marks were much bigger than that of any discovered squid species.

55.   Situated on Sark Island in Guernsey, an island between England and France, Sark Prison is the world's smallest prison which only fits two people.

56.   In 2010, a man got lost in the woods of northern Saskatchewan and chopped down power lines just to draw attention to himself, in hopes that someone would rescue him. It worked.

57.   The longest that anyone has ever survived in a shipwrecked raft was 133 days by a Chinese man named Poon Lim in 1942. He survived by fishing, drinking bird blood, and even killing a shark with a jug of water. He lived to the age of seventy two, dying in 1991.

58.   In Tunisia, you can book an overnight stay at Luke Skywalker's boyhood home, which is a real hotel called "Hotel Sidi Driss," for only $10.

59.   In 2011, the Coble family lost their three children, two girls and a boy, in an unfortunate car accident. A year later the mother gave birth to triplets, two girls and one boy.

Animals

60.   In 2013, it was discovered that some bears in Russia have become addicted to sniffing jet fuel out of discarded barrels. They even go to the lengths of stalking helicopters for the drops of fuel that they leave behind.

61.   Humans are not appropriate prey for great white sharks because their digestion is too slow to cope with the ratio of bone to muscle and fat.

62.   The Savannah is the largest domestic breed of cats which resembles a small leopard but behaves like a dog. They can grow up to forty pounds (eighteen kilograms), have an eight foot (2.4 meter) vertical jump, and be trained to walk on a leash and play fetch.

63.   Flamingos are born grey but change to the pink color we see because of the shrimp they eat which dyes their feathers.

64.   The only bird that can fly backwards is the hummingbird.

65.   In real life, a roadrunner can only reach speeds of about twenty miles (thirty two kilometers) per hour while a coyote can reach speeds of up to forty three miles (sixty nine kilometers) per hour.

66.   The "Orca," also known as the killer whale, actually belongs to the dolphin family.

67.   It's possible for a cat to be its own fraternal twin. These cats, known as "Chimera cats," are an oddity that occur when two fertilized eggs fuse together.

68.   One third of the world's polar bear population lives in Canada.

69.   Hippos sweat the color red because it contains a pigment that acts as a natural sunscreen.

70. Raccoons are extremely intelligent creatures. They can open complex locks in under ten tries and even repeat the process if the locks are rearranged or turned upside down. They can also remember solutions to problems for up to three years.

71. Cows' methane creates just as much pollution as cars do.

72. Dolphins only fall asleep with half their brain at a time so they're only half conscious, which helps them from accidentally drowning.

73. Snails can sleep for up to three years.

74. The average shark has fifteen rows of teeth in each jaw. They can replace a tooth in a single day and lose over 30,000 teeth in their lifetime.

75. There are completely black chickens in Indonesia known as Ayam Cemani. They have black plumage, legs, nails, beak, tongue, comb, wattle, and even black meat, bones and organs.

76. Christmas Island is a small Australian island located in the Indian Ocean that every year sees fifty million adult crabs migrate from the forest to breed. It's known as the annual red crab migration.

77. A flamingo can only eat when its head is upside down.

78. Starbuck is a famous Canadian bull whose genome is so desirable that his sperm has sold for over twenty five million dollars over his lifetime. In this time he has sired over 200,000 daughters.

79. Giraffes can last longer without water than camels can.

80. Elephants are constantly tip toeing around. This is because the back of their foot has no bone and is all fat.

81. An octopus has nine brains, blue blood, and three hearts.

82. Polar bears' hair is actually clear and it's the light they reflect that makes them appear to look white.

83. A chameleon can move its eyes two different directions at the same time.

84. In one night, a mole can dig a tunnel 300 feet (one kilometer) long in soil.

85. The age of fish can be determined in a similar way to trees. Fish scales have one growth ring for each year of age.

86. Fully grown giraffes only have seven vertebrae in their necks, the same number as humans.

87. When bats are born, they come out feet first, and in many cases, the mother bat hangs

upside down so she can catch the baby in her wings as it exits the womb.

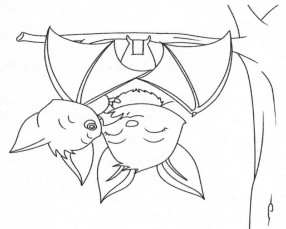

88. In 2007, in Louisiana, a pink albino bottlenose dolphin was discovered and photographed by a man named Eric Rue.

89. When the elephant whisperer Lawrence Anthony died in March of 2012, an entire herd of elephants arrived at his home to mourn him.

90. Ostriches have eyes bigger than their heads.

91. If gorillas take human birth control pills, it will have the same effects on them.

92. Koalas can sleep up to eighteen to twenty two hours a day, whereas a giraffe only needs about two.

93. Fleas can jump over eighty times their own height.

94. Rhinoceros beetles can carry 850 times their weight, which is the equivalent of an average human carrying sixty five tons.

95. The black mamba is regarded as one of the deadliest snakes in the world. It can move up to speeds of eighteen feet (5.5 meters) per second and its bite can kill a human in less than an hour.

96. Woodpeckers are able to peck twenty times per second or around 8,000 to 12,000 pecks per day without ever getting a headache.

97. Sea otters hold hands when they sleep so they don't drift away from each other.

98. Most cats don't like to drink water if it's too close to their food source. Always keep your cat's water and food supply separate so they don't get dehydrated.

99. Jellyfish and lobsters are biologically immortal.

100. Cows have best friends and can be stressed when separated from them.

101. Cats don't meow to each other, they meow to get the attention of humans.

102. Snails have the ability to regrow an eye if it's cut off.

103. A penguin has the ability to jump six feet (1.8 meters) out of the water with no aid.

104. Honey badgers have been known to eat porcupines and poisonous snakes, raid bee hives for honey, kidnap baby cheetahs, and steal food from hungry lions.

105. Beaver eyelids are transparent so they can see through them as they swim underwater.

106. Adult cats don't have enough lactase enzyme to digest the lactose from milk making them lactose intolerant.

107. Koi fish can live for centuries. The oldest Koi to have ever lived was one named Hanako that lived for 225 years before it died.

108. A blue whale can consume 480 million calories of food in a single dive.

109. Ants go to war just like humans and they can, in fact, strategize by doing things like sending out the weaker ants to fight first.

110. A giraffe's tongue is eight inches (twenty one centimeters) long.

111. It would take 1.2 million mosquitoes sucking once each to completely drain the blood in a human adult.

112. Lions have the loudest roar of any animal reaching 114 decibels at a distance of about 3.2 feet (one meter). It can be heard from over two miles (three kilometers) away.

113. Sloths can live up to thirty years and spend fifteen to eighteen hours a day sleeping.

114. When the silk of a spider is stored in its body, it's actually liquid; it only hardens and becomes solid when it leaves the spider's glands and comes into contact with the air.

115. Mosquitoes don't just bite you and suck your blood, they urinate on you before flying off.

116. The largest living beings ever to have lived on Earth are blue whales. Their tongues alone can weigh as much as an elephant and their hearts as much as a car.

117. Humans have the largest brain in terms of brain to body ratio. The animal with the biggest brain overall is a sperm whale weighing in at seventeen pounds (seven kilograms).

118. Besides the crocodile's belly and top of its head, the rest of the skin is bulletproof.

119. In 2001, a lion cub, bear cub, and tiger cub were found abandoned in a drug dealer's basement. They were soon adopted by a sanctuary and have lived together ever since.

120. There's a chimpanzee in a Russian zoo named Zhora that became addicted to booze and smoking after too many visitors began giving him alcoholic treats and cigarettes. In 2001, the chimp actually had to be sent to rehab to be treated for his addictions.

121. In 2006, a rare grizzly and polar bear hybrid species was confirmed in Canada called "pizzly bears" or "grolar bears." Global warming is causing polar bears habitats to melt so they find shelter elsewhere and end up mating with grizzlies.

122. Crocodiles cannot stick out their tongues or chew.

123. In order to drink, giraffes have to spread their almost 6.5 feet (two meter) long legs apart just to get close enough to the water.

124. Bed bugs survive longer in beds that are made, so scientists actually suggest that you leave your bed unmade once in a while as it ends up being healthier for you.

125. Pandas are the national animals of China. They are also only found in this country, and if you happen to see one in another country, they're on loan there.

126. A grizzly bear's jaw strength is so powerful that it could crush a bowling bowl with it.

127. A leopon is a hybrid animal cross between a male leopard and a lioness.

128. Sand tiger shark embryos fight each other to the death within the mother's womb until there's one survivor, which is the one that gets to be born.

129. There is an insect called the "assassin bug" which wears its victim's corpse as armor.

130. There was a golden haired Tibetan Mastiff puppy which sold for twelve million yuan, or two million dollars, making it the most expensive dog in the world.

131. Unlike many other members of the cat family, tigers actually enjoy water and can swim well. They often soak in streams or pools of water to cool off.

132. The skin of a honey badger is so thick that it can withstand machete blows, arrows, and spears. The only sure way to kill one is by using a club or a gun.

133. Dolphins don't drink seawater as it makes them ill or could even potentially kill them. Instead they get all their liquids from the food that they eat.

134. There are giant hornets in Japan with venom so strong that it can melt human skin.

135. Rabbits are able to sleep with their eyes open. They go into a trance-like state, which makes them only half asleep. The advantage of this is that, in the wild, it allows them to be more alert and get away from predators in a hurry.

136. It takes twelve bees a lifetime of work to create a teaspoon of honey.

137. There used to be horse sized ducks called "dromornithidae" roaming around present day Australia 50,000 years ago.

138. Camels have three eyelids that protects them from the rough winds in deserts.

139. Due to the placement of a donkey's eyes, it can see all four of its feet at all times.

140. Slugs have tentacles, blowholes, and thousands of teeth.

141. In praying mantises, 25% of all sexual encounters result in the death of the male as the female begins by ripping the male's head off.

142. The loneliest animal in the world is a male whale in the North Pacific which can't find a mate due to the way it communicates. The whale's frequency is on another level and can't be heard by other whales.

143. Depending on the species of sharks, they can either give birth to live young or lay eggs.

144. A cockroach can live up to several weeks without its head. It only dies due to hunger.

145. A man in Wisconsin took a photo containing three albino deer in the woods. The chances of this happening is one in seventy nine billion.

146. An elephant drinks thirty four gallons (130 liters) of water a day.

147. Skunks have muscles next to their scent glands that allow them to spray their fluids accurately up to ten feet (three meters) away.

148. There are fifty different types of kangaroos.

149. Between the 1600's and 1800's, lobsters were known as the cockroaches of the sea. They were fed to prisoners and servants and were used as fish bait.

150. There is a super tiny species of antelope called the "Dick-Dick," named after the sound they make when alarmed.

151. Termites are currently being researched by scientists at UConn and Caltech as possible renewable energy sources. They can produce up to half a gallon (two liters) of hydrogen by ingesting a single sheet of paper, making them one of the planet's most efficient bio-reactors.

152. In Japan, there are owl cafes where you can play with live owls while enjoying a drink or meal.

153. Cats are one of the only animals that domesticate themselves and approach humans on their own terms.

154. When ants die, they secrete a chemical that tells other ants to move the body to a sort of burial ground. If this chemical is sprayed on a live ant, other ants will treat it as a dead ant, regardless of what it does.

155. Australia is home to the golden silk orb weave spiders, arachnids that are so big that they can eat entire foot and a half (half meter) long snakes.

156. There was a goat in Utah named Freckles that was implanted with spider genes as an embryo and it's now known as the Spider Goat. She produces spider silk proteins in her milk, which is used to make bio-steel, a material stronger than Kevlar.

157. There is an insect called "the tree lobster" which is almost the size of a human hand. They can only be found in one place, on the huge mountainous remains of an old volcano called "Ball's Island" off the coast of Australia.

158. Naked mole rats are one of the only animals to not get cancer.

159. Crocodiles don't have sweat glands. In order to cool themselves down, they keep their jaws open.

160. Crows have the ability to recognize human faces and even hold grudges against the ones they don't like.

161. Jaguars in the wild are known for frequently getting high by eating hallucinogenic roots, which also increase their senses for hunting.

162. Prairie dogs say hello with kisses.

163. The smallest poisonous frog is only ten millimeters in length and it secretes a toxic poison from its skin as a defense mechanism.

164. A scorpion can hold its breath underwater for up to six days.

165. There's a fish called the black dragon fish that looks very similar to the creature from the Alien movies.

166. The reason birds fly in a "V" formation is to save energy due to wind resistance. The birds take turns being in the front and fall to the back when they're tired.

167. The African driver ant can produce three to four million eggs every twenty five days.

168. Polar bears evolved from brown bears somewhere in the vicinity of Britain and Ireland 150,000 years ago.

169. The fastest land animal is the cheetah which has a recorded speed of seventy five miles (120 kilometers) per hour.

170. A jellyfish has no ears, eyes, nose, brain, or heart.

171. If two rats were left alone in an enclosed area with enough room, they can multiply to a million within eighteen months.

172. Crabs are able to regenerate their legs and claws to 95% of their original size.

173. A camel can drink fifty three gallons (200 liters) of water in three minutes.

174. Male puppies will let female puppies win when they play, even though they are physically more powerful, to encourage them to play more.

175. An Indiana state prison allows murderers to adopt cats in their cells to help teach them love and compassion for other living things.

176. The infinite monkey theorem states that a monkey hitting keys at random on a typewriter for an infinite amount of time will eventually type out any given text, including the complete works of William Shakespeare.

177. Cockroaches were here 120 million years before the dinosaurs.

178. The most popular animal for a pet is freshwater fish. Next comes the cat followed by the dog.

179. Baboons in the wild have been known to kidnap puppies and raise them as pets.

180. The smallest known reptile in the world is the Brookesia micra, which is so small it can stand on the head of a match.

181. In Moscow, stray dogs have learned to commute from the suburbs to the city, scavenge for food, then catch the train home in the evening.

182. There was an orangutan named Fu Manchu who was repeatedly able to escape from his cage at the Henry Doorly Zoo in Nebraska. It was found that he was using a key that he fashioned out of a piece of wire. The reason he was able to do it so many times and kept getting away with it was because every time the zookeeper's inspected him, he would hide the key in his mouth.

183. Pigs are physically incapable to look up into the sky.

184. There are over 1,200 different species of bats in the world, and contrary to popular belief, none of them are blind. Bats can hunt in the dark using echolocation, which means they use echoes of self-produced sounds bouncing off objects to help them navigate.

185. In 2006, a study done by Alex Thornton and Katherine McAuliffe at Cambridge University showed how adult meerkats teach their youngest pups how not to be stung by scorpions, one of their main sources of prey. First, they bring dead scorpions to the pups; then they bring ones that are alive but injured; and, eventually, they work their way up to live prey.

186. Most of the camels in Saudi Arabia are imported from Australia.

187. China is home to half of the pig population on earth.

188. There are 1.2 million species documented in existence today, however, scientists estimate the number to be somewhere around 8.7 million. Due to extinction, however, we may never know the exact number.

189. Grasshoppers have ears in the sides of their abdomen.

190. There are miniature wolves in the Middle East that only reach about thirty pounds (six kilograms). In comparison, the largest wolves in the world found in Canada, Russia, and Alaska can reach up to 175 pounds (eighty kilograms).

191. There's a dog named Faith that was born with no front legs but learned to walk on its hind legs. The dog and its owner both travel to military hospitals to demonstrate that even a dog with a severe disability can live a full life.

192. There's a thirty four year old chimpanzee named Kanzi that not only knows how to start a fire and cook food, but knows how to make omelets for himself.

193. There is a lake in the country of Palau called "Jellyfish Lake" where jellyfish have evolved without stingers. These golden jellyfish are completely harmless to humans and you can even swim with them.

194. In 1997, a seventeen year old Merino sheep named Shrek, in New Zealand, ran away and hid in a cave for seven years. When he was finally found in 2004, he had gone unsheared for so long that he had accumulated sixty pounds (twenty seven kilograms) of wool on his body, the equivalent to make twenty suits.

195. Mike, the Headless Chicken, was a famous chicken from 1945 that was beheaded by a farmer for his dinner but continued to live for another eighteen full months.

196. Lobsters taste with their feet. The tiny bristles inside a lobster's little pincers are their equivalent to human taste buds.

197. ManhattAnts are an ant species unique to New York City. Biologists found them in a specific 14-block strip of the city.

198. All dogs are banned from Antarctica since April 1994. This ban was made because of the concern that dogs might spread diseases to seals.

Art & Artists

199. A Dutch artist discovered a way to create clouds in the middle of a room by carefully balancing humidity, lighting, and temperature. He uses this regularly in his artwork.

200. Xylography is the art of engraving on wood.

201. The well-known Leonardo da Vinci was a huge lover of animals. In fact, he was a vegetarian and was also known to buy birds from markets only to set them free.

202. A Mexican artist created an underwater sculpture series that double as art and an artificial reef.

203. There is a method of art called "tree shaping" where living trees are manipulated to create forms of art.

204. The singing tree is a wind powered sound sculpture located in Burnley, England, and was designed by architects Mike Tonkin and Anna Liu. Each time you sit under it, you'll hear a melody played depending on the wind for that day.

205. The Mona Lisa has no eyelashes or eyebrows.

206. In 1961, Italian artist Piero Manzoni filled ninety tin cans of his own feces, called them "Artist's sh*t," and sold them according to their equivalent weight in gold.

207. In China, there is a 233 foot (seventy one meter) tall stone statue built of Buddha that was constructed over 1,200 years ago.

208. The famous painter Salvador Dali would avoid paying the bill at restaurants by drawing on the back of his checks. He knew the owner wouldn't want to cash the checks as the drawings would be too valuable.

209. There's an artist named Scott Wade who is famous for creating dust art on dirty cars using only his fingers and a brush.

210. In the Curve Gallery at the Barbican Center in London, there's something called "the rain room" where through the use of sensors, rain falls everywhere in the room except for where you're walking.

211. Instead of using spray cans, some artists create semi-permanent images on walls or other places by removing dirt from a surface. It's known as reverse graffiti or clean tagging.

212. There's a Turkish artist named Esref Armagan who is blind, yet taught himself to write and paint and has been doing so on his own for the last thirty five years.

213. In Mexico, artists like painters, sculptors, and graphic artists can pay their taxes by donating pieces of artwork that they create to the government.

214. In 2006, artist Kim Graham and a group of twenty five volunteers spent fifteen days using entirely non-toxic recycled paper products to create a twelve foot (3.7 meter) tall paper mache tree doll.

215. There's an artist named Brian Lai that has the unique ability to draw in negatives.

216. The Terracotta Army is a collection of more than 8,000 clay soldiers, chariots, and horses that took around thirty seven years to make. They were buried with the Emperor in 210 B.C. with the purpose of protecting him in his afterlife.

217. Michelangelo wrote a poem about how much he hated painting the Sistine Chapel.

218. Eight of the ten largest statues in the world are of Buddhas.

219. The three wise monkeys actually have names. The see no evil monkey is named Mizaru, the hear no evil monkey is named Mikazaru, and the speak no evil monkey is named Mazaru.

Bizare

220. In London, there's a public toilet encased in a glass cube that's made entirely of one-way glass where you can see passersby, but they can't see you.

221. It's possible to hire an evil clown to terrorize your son or daughter for an entire week before their birthday. For a fee, artist Dominic Deville will increasingly pursue your child and leave scary notes, texts, and phone calls, and ultimately attack your child on their birthday by smashing a cake in their face.

222. In response to China's worsening air pollution, a Chinese millionaire started selling cans of fresh air for the price of eighty cents a can. Incredibly, he made over six million dollars.

223. The longest someone has stayed awake continuously is 265 hours, which was in 1964 by a high school student.

224. There are now snuggery services where you can hire someone to snuggle with you for $60 per hour.

225. In Switzerland, if you fail your practical driver's license three times, you are required to consult an official psychologist to assess the reason for your previous failures before you're allowed to retake the exam.

226. There is a Japanese practice known

as "forest bathing" where you just hang out around trees. It's proven to lower blood pressure, heart rate, reduce stress, boost your immune system, and increase your overall well being.

227. You are not allowed to flush the toilet after 10 p.m. in Switzerland. Other bizarre things you can't do in this country are: using a high-pressure power hose on your car, hiking naked, hanging out laundry, cutting your grass, or recycling on Sundays. Some random things you must do in this country are paying tax on your dog if you have one and having a buddy for pets such as guinea pigs, gold fish, and budgies so they have company.

228. Outside of Watson Lake, Yukon, there's a Sign Post Forest. It was started back in 1942 when a soldier named Carl K. Lindley was injured while working on the Alcan Highway. He was taken to the Army air station in Watson Lake to recover, and while he was there, he was homesick, so he decided to place a sign of Danville, Illinois, his hometown. Tourists continued the practice and there are currently about 72,000 signs from around the world.

Books, Comic Books & Writers

229. The creator of Sherlock Holmes, Sir Arthur Conan Doyle, helped to get two falsely accused men out of prison after solving their already closed cases.

230. There are Wizard of Oz-inspired shoes that get you home when clicking your heels together using a GPS system. Side note: the author of the novel created part of the name of the book when he was looking at a filing cabinet and saw the letters o-z.

231. There are three books in the Harvard University that are bound in human skin.

232. Yale has a rare book and manuscript library that has no windows, but instead it has walls made entirely of translucent marble that prevents the books from being exposed to direct sunlight.

233. Author J. K. Rowling wrote the final chapter of the last Harry Potter book in 1990, seven years before the release of the first book.

234. The children's book "Where the Wild Things Are" was originally titled "Where the Wild Horses Are," however, the author and illustrator Maurice Sendak ended up changing the name of it after he realized he had no idea how to draw horses.

235. The best selling book in history is the Bible with five billion copies in sales.

236. DC Comics published an alternate universe where Bruce Wayne dies instead of his parents. In it, Thomas Wayne becomes Batman and Martha Wayne goes crazy and becomes the Joker.

237. The first ever occurrence of the name "Wendy" was in Peter Pan. This name had never been registered before the book's publication.

238. There is an ancient book called "The Voynich" from the Italian Renaissance that no one can read.

239. In 1994, Leonardo da Vinci's Codex Leicester notebook was bought by Bill Gates for $30.8 million. Besides adding the item to his personal collection, he used it to also help promote Windows Vista's launch, by using a program called Turning the Pages 2.0 that would let people browse through virtual versions of the notebook.

240. In 1983, Marvel published a comic called "Your Friendly Neighborhood Spider Ham." The character was a spider pig named Peter Porker.

241. There's a book that exists called "Everything Men know about Woman" that has 100 pages all of which are blank.

242. In 1975, Professor Jack Hetherington from Michigan State University added his cat as a co-author to a theoretical paper that he had been working on. He did this because he mistakenly used words like "we" and "our" in the paper and didn't feel like revising it.

243. There is a Russian published novel called the "Last Ringbearer" which retells the Lord of the Rings from the perspective of Sauron.

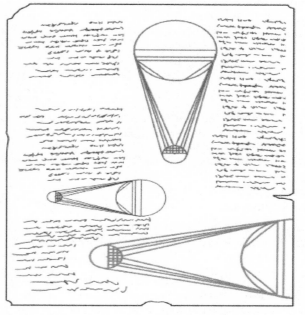

244. The letter "u" was first used as a substitute for the word "you" by William Shakespeare in his comedy "Love's Labour's Lost" around 1595.

245. In 1996, DC and Marvel Comics published a crossover series where Wolverine and Batman were made into one character called "Dark Claw" or "Logan Wayne."

246. Although the Holy Bible is available for free at many places of worship, it is the most stolen book in the world.

247. In the original version of "The Little Mermaid" by Hans Christian Anderson, Ariel doesn't marry the prince. She actually marries someone else and she dies.

248. In the early versions of the "Little Red Riding Hood," the girl cannibalizes her own grandmother and then gets eaten by the wolf after getting into bed with him.

249. The original script of Lord of the Rings was one long saga, but it was split into three books for the publishers to make more money.

250. The code of Hammurabi is a well preserved Babylonian law that dates all the way back to 1772 B.C. which had progressive laws in it such as minimum wage and the right to be a free man. It was written well before the Bible.

251. Adult coloring books are becoming a huge trend and publishers actually struggle to

keep up with demand. The books seem to be a way to successfully reduce stress and relieve anxiety. They are even used as rehabilitation aids for patients who are recovering from strokes.

252. In the novel Forrest Gump that the movie was based upon, Forrest goes into space with NASA but upon returning, he crash lands on an island full of cannibals and only manages to survive by beating the head cannibal every day at chess.

253. Journalist Sara Bongiorni and her family attempted to live without Chinese-made goods for an entire year and found it almost impossible. They documented their experience in a book called "A year without 'made in China'."

254. Richard Klinkhamer, a Dutch crime writer, wrote a suspicious book on seven ways to kill your spouse, one year after his wife disappeared. He became a celebrity and spent the next decade hinting that he murdered her, and in 2000, it turned out that he really had after her skeleton was discovered at his former residence.

255. The reason Harry Potter and the Goblet of Fire is longer than the first three books is because author J.K. Rowling made a plot hole half way through and had to go back and fix it.

256. The Old Testament was written over the course of 1,000 years whereas the New Testament was written within seventy five years.

257. Before the renaissance era, three quarters of all books in the world were in Chinese.

258. J.K. Rowling is the first author to reach billionaire status. She also holds the status of losing her billionaire status due to giving away most of her money.

Buildings & Massive Monuments

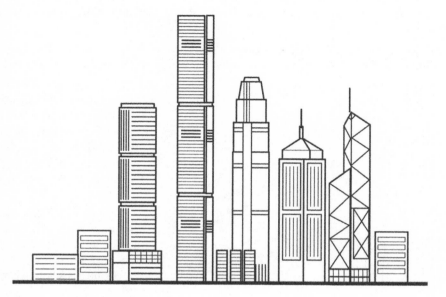

259. It took over twenty two centuries to complete the Great Wall of China. It was built, rebuilt, and extended by many imperial dynasties and kingdoms. The wall exceeds 12,000 miles (20,000 kilometers).

260. There's a building in London called the "Walkie Talkie Building" that's shaped in such a way that it reflects sunlight like a giant magnifying glass, literally melting cars on the street below.

261. The Lego-Brucke is a concrete bridge in Germany that has become famous for being painted to look like a giant bridge made of Lego blocks.

262. The world's largest tree house is located in Tennessee and is ten stories, 10,000 square feet (900 square meters), took eleven years to make, but it cost only $12,000 since it was made of mostly recycled materials.

263. The Pyramid of Giza was built from two million stone bricks with stones weighing more than two tons each. It was built over the course of eighty five years.

264. There is a sixteen story office building in Osaka, Japan, called "The Gate Tower Building" that has an entire highway that passes through the fifth, sixth, and seventh floors of the structure.

265. In 2014, Budapest broke the world record for the tallest Lego tower ever built. Made of 450,000 colorful bricks, topped with a large Hungarian Rubik's cube, the structure stands at 114 feet (thirty four meters) tall in front of Saint Stephen's Basilica.

266. In 2013, Vietnam unveiled a steel bridge that's shaped like a dragon that literally shoots fire out of its mouth; it's called the "Dragon Bridge."

267. The world's largest privately constructed nuclear fallout shelter is the "Ark Two." It began being built in the 1980's by Bruce Beach just north of Toronto. It's ten thousand square feet (929 square meters) and is composed of forty two school buses mixed with concrete, runs on internal generators, and has its own chapel, decontamination room, and radio station.

268. Some buildings in the US, such as the White House, the Empire State Building, the Sears Building, and the Dodger Stadium, are so large that they have their own zip codes.

269. Even though the Eiffel Tower is stable on its four legs, it is known to move. The 900 foot (320 meter) structure can sway if the wind is strong enough or expand seven inches (17.7 centimeters) if the sun is hot enough.

270. The Burj Khalifa is the tallest building in the world standing at 2,700 feet (830 meters). Construction started in 2004 and took four years to complete.

271. Until its demolition in 2012, 1% of Greenland's entire population lived in one apartment building called "Blok P."

272. The most expensive thing ever created is the International Space Station at a cost of $160 billion and rising as new sections are added.

273. There is a skywalk on Tianmen Mountain, in China, which is a 200 feet (sixty one meters) long with 8.2 feet (2.5 meter) thick glass. The bridge is so high up that it allows visitors to look down on the peaks of smaller mountains below.

274. The "Intempo" skyscraper in Spain has forty seven floors but no elevators.

275. The first building to have more than 100 floors was the Empire State Building.

Cool

276. Thailand celebrates a festival each year named Loy Krathong where they release thousands upon thousands of sky lanterns filling up the night sky as tradition.

277. When Stephen Hawking was asked what his IQ was, he responded: "I have no idea, but people who boast about their IQ are losers."

278. There is a cruise ship named "The World" where residents permanently live as it travels around the globe. An apartment on board costs $2 million while you fork out $270,000 a year for maintenance costs.

279. China is building a car free city called "The Great City" that will house 80,000 people. It'll use 48% less energy, 58% less water, produce 89% less landfill waste, and 60% less carbon dioxide than a conventional city of the same size.

280. Harris Rosen was a self-made millionaire that decided to fund a small neighborhood named "Tangelo Park." Harris helped reduce the crime rate by over 50% and increased graduation for high school from 20% to 100% by giving everyone free child care and scholarships.

281. The Burj Al Arab Hotel in Dubai offers their guests a twenty four karat gold iPad for the duration of their stay.

282. There's a vending machine in Singapore that dispenses a Coke to anybody that hugs it.

283. Newman's Own Food has donated 100% of its post-tax profits to charity since 1982, totaling over $400 million.

284. There's a resort in Japan called the "Tomamu Resort" that's located on top of a mountain peak that allows patrons to view a sea of fluffy white clouds beneath them.

285. In the UK, people that reach their 100th birthday or their 60th wedding anniversary are sent a personalized card from the Queen.

286. The oldest hotel in the world is the "Nishiyama Onsen Keiunkan" in Japan. It was founded in 705 A.D. and has had fifty two generations of the same family operating it since it was founded.

287. In Australia, there is a bookstore where books are wrapped in paper with short descriptions. This way they are buying a book without judging it by its cover.

288. There is man named Tim Harris with Down syndrome who owns and runs a restaurant in Albuquerque, New Mexico, called "Tim's Place," where they serve breakfast, lunch, and hugs. It's the only known restaurant owned by a person with Down syndrome and it's known as the world's friendliest restaurant.

289. Dalhousie University in Halifax, Nova Scotia, has opened a puppy room where students can go play with puppies to relieve stress.

290. Former billionaire Chuck Feeney has given away over 99% of his $6.3 billion to help underprivileged kids go to college resulting in him having $2 million left.

291. Every factory employee at Ben and Jerry's gets to take home three pints of ice cream every day.

292. A 102 year old man named Alan Swift, from Connecticut, drove the same 1928 Rolls Royce Phantom 1 for close to seventy seven years before he died in 2005.

293. In 2005, Johan Eliasch, a Swedish millionaire, bought a plot of land almost half a million acres big in the Amazon rainforest just so he could preserve it.

294. The largest indoor water park in the world is the Seagaia Ocean Dome in Japan at 900 feet (300 meters) long and 328 feet (100 meters) wide.

295. In 2011, Barack Obama became the first president to have ever brewed beer in the White House; the beer was named "White House Honey Ale."

296. In Finland, when you earn your PhD, you're given a doctoral hat that looks like a top hat as well as a doctoral sword.

297. There's a school called "Ordinary Miracle" in Yoshkar-Ola, Russia, that looks like a fairy-tale castle. A man named Sergey Mamaev had built it for his wife who wanted to teach at a school that children would actually want to go to.

298. The small pocket in your large pocket of your jeans was originally meant for your

pocket watch.

299. In March 2013, a man got a tattoo of the word Netflix on his side for which, after tweeting a picture of it to the company, gave him a free year of service.

300. At the Crocosaurus Cove Aquarium in Australia, there's a popular tourist attraction called the "Cage of Death" which allows you to get up close and personal with giant crocodiles.

301. There is a luxury hotel in Fiji called "Poseidon Resort" where, for $15,000 a week, you can sleep on the ocean floor and even get a button to feed the fish right outside your window.

302. Photographer Andrew Suryono was under heavy rain when he noticed an orangutan using a leaf for shelter. He quickly took the shot that made him earn an honorable mention in the 2015 National Geographic photo contest.

303.   There's a Canadian toy company called "Child's Own Studios" that turns children's drawings into stuffed animals.

304.   There's an alarm clock named Clocky that has wheels and runs away and hides if you don't get out of bed on time.

305.   Norway allows any student from anywhere in the world to study at their public universities completely free of charge.

306.   Tourists throw over a million euros into the Trevi Fountain in Rome each year. The city uses this money to fund a supermarket for the poor.

307. Henry Ford was the first industrial giant to give his workers both Saturday and Sunday off in hopes that it would encourage more leisure use of vehicles, hence popularizing the concept of the weekend.

308. Lamborghinis, Bentleys, Aston Martins are all used as police cars in Dubai.

309. The "Santa Rita do Sapucai" prison in Brazil allows its inmates to pedal exercise bikes to power lights in a nearby town in exchange for reduced sentences. For every sixteen hours that they pedal, one day is reduced from their sentence.

310. In 2012, a man in China named Zao Phen had 9,999 red roses sewn into a dress for his girlfriend before asking for her hand in marriage.

311. There is a house sized shoe box in Amsterdam that is an Adidas store.

312. Sweden recycles so well that it actually has to import garbage from Norway in order to fuel its waste to power energy plants.

313. There is a swing at the edge of a cliff in Ecuador that has no safety measures. It hangs from a tree house overlooking an active volcano called the "Swing at the End of the World."

314. In the University of Victoria in British Columbia, Canada, you can take a course in the science of Batman. It uses the caped crusader to explain the human condition and the limitations of the human mind and body.

315. In Chongqing, China, there is a zoo called the "Lehe Ledu Wildlife Zoo" where visitors are placed in cages instead of the animals. The cages are stalked by lions and tigers, so the guests are warned to keep their fingers and hands inside the cage at all times.

316. On the first day of school, children in Germany, Austria, and the Czech Republic are given a cardboard cone filled with toys and sweets known as a Schultute.

317. The deepest indoor pool is located in Brussels, Belgium, named "Nemo 33" at 108 feet (thirty two meters) deep.

318. The WWOOF, or the Worldwide Opportunities on Organic Farms, is an international program that allows you to travel the world with free food and accommodation in exchange for volunteer work.

319. In 2007, a twin was born thirty four minutes after her brother, but because of a daylight savings time adjustment, she was actually born twenty six minutes before her brother.

320. George Barbe, a billionaire from Alabama, had several life sized dinosaurs built and placed over his ten thousand acre home in 1991.

321. In 2013, a company called "Limite Zero" created a 2,300 foot (720 meter) international zip-line between Spain and Portugal.

322. It's estimated that there are approximately three million shipwrecks on the ocean floor worth billions of dollars in value and treasure.

323. Mark Zuckerberg has signed the "Giving Pledge," a campaign created by Warren Buffet and Bill Gates which encourages wealthy people to contribute the majority of their wealth to

philanthropic causes.

324. In 1993, Dave Thomas, the founder of Wendy's, went back to high school to earn his GED decades after dropping out because he was worried kids may see his success as an excuse to also drop out of school.

325. The Technical University of Munich built slides four stories high to help their students get to class quickly instead of them having to take the stairs.

326. The Canadian post office has assigned a postal code of H, O, H, O, H, O, to the North Pole where anyone can send a letter to Santa Claus. Every year more than one million letters are addressed to Santa Claus, each of which are answered in the same language they were written in.

327. Tap water in Canada is regulated to a higher standard than bottled water.

328. In Siberia, there's a toilet located 8,500 feet (2,591 meters) above sea level at the top of the Altai Mountains. It serves the workers of an isolated weather station and is known as the world's loneliest toilet.

329. On Marajo Island, Brazilian police ride water buffalos when they patrol the streets instead of horses.

Countries & Cities

330. In Cuba, it's legally mandated that government vehicles must pick up any hitchhikers that they see.

331. The heaviest drinkers in the world are in Belarus with 17.5 liters consumed per capita every year.

332. The distance between Africa and Europe is only fourteen miles (twenty three kilometers.) There are talks of constructing a bridge between the two continents called the "Strait of Gibraltar Crossing."

333. The country with the most millionaires is the US. The country with the most billionaires is China.

334. There's a village in the Netherlands named Giethoorn that has no roads and can only be accessed by boats, having the nickname "Venice of the Netherlands."

335. Poveglia Island, in Italy, is considered one of the most haunted places in the world as it was the site of wars, a dumping ground for plague victims, and an insane asylum. In fact, it's so haunted that the Italian government has forbidden public access to it.

336. France is the only country in Europe to be completely self-sufficient in basic food production.

337. In the country of Turkilometersenistan, water, gas, and electricity have all been free from the government since 1993.

338. The whole country of England is smaller than the state of Florida by over 10,000 square miles (26,000 square kilometers).

339. In an effort to fight obesity, the government from Mexico City offers a free subway ticket to each person who does ten squats. Currently, 70% of the adult population is overweight.

340. It has only snowed in Cuba once, back in March 12, 1857.

341. There are 158 verses in the national anthem of Greece making it the longest in the world. In comparison, the Canadian anthem only has four verses.

342. In Iceland, if you want to give your baby a name that's never been used before, you must go to the Icelandic Naming Committee.

343. In the city of Mackinac Island, Michigan, all motor vehicles including cars have been banned since 1898.

344. Geographically, China covers five different times zones, however, only one standard time zone within the country is used.

345. Citizens of Norway only pay half their taxes in November so they can have more money for Christmas.

346. The state of Illinois has banned exfoliating face washes because the microbeads in them are so small that they actually slip through the water treatment facilities and end up back in the water supply.

347. The Indonesian Ministry of Marine Affairs and Fisheries determined that a single manta ray, if caught and killed, is worth anywhere from $40-$500. They also determined, however, that if kept alive, they're worth up to a million dollars in tourism revenue. They created the largest manta ray sanctuary in the world.

348. The longest street in the world is Yonge Street in Canada which is 1,178 miles (1,896 kilometers) long.

349. There is no explanation why there are no mosquitoes in Iceland.

350. Cuba has the highest doctor to patient ratio in the world.

351. The highest divorce rate in the world by country is Luxembourg at 87%. The lowest is India with 1%.

352. 99.8% of Cubans can read and write making it one of the most literate countries in the world.

353. Indonesia has more than 17,000 islands.

354. There are more vegetarians in India than in any other country.

355. If you left Tokyo by plane at 7 a.m., you would arrive at Honolulu at approximately 8 p.m. the previous day due to the nineteen hour difference in time zone.

356. The country with the longest coastline on Earth is Canada.

357. Since 1979, no one has been reported to die from a confirmed spider bite in Australia.

Deaths by spiders actually occur more when you are surprised by them, e.g. when you are driving.

358. The first country where a woman was allowed to vote was New Zealand in 1893.

359. In 2013, Google sent a lone employee to an abandoned Japanese island called "Gunkjima" to map it for Google Street View. The island was once the most densely populated island in the world, but it's now completely abandoned.

360. Switzerland has enough nuclear shelters to accommodate 114% of its population. It's a legal requirement for the Swiss to have a protected place that can be reached quickly from their place of residence.

361. Iceland has no army and has been recognized as the most peaceful country in the world for the last six years. In comparison, the UK is forty four, and the US sits at 100.

362. There are zero rivers in Saudi Arabia.

363. There is a city called "Rome" in each continent.

364. In Egypt, actors were once not allowed to testify in court as they were seen as professional liars.

365. Over 90% of the Australian population live within fifty kilometers of its coastline.

366. In the state of Nevada, public intoxication is not only explicitly legal, but it's illegal for any city or town to pass a law making it illegal.

367. In Churchill Manitoba, Canada, it's illegal to lock your car in case someone needs to hide from one of the 900 polar bears in the area.

368. The Okinawa Island in Japan has over four hundred people living above the age of 100 and it's known as the healthiest place on earth.

369. Germany was the first country to realize the link between smoking and lung cancer. Hitler was even one of the first ones to lead the anti-smoking campaign.

370. The Philippine island of Luzon contains a lake that contains an island that contains a lake that contains another island.

371. License plates in the Canadian Northwest territories are shaped like polar bears.

372. The largest cemetery in the world is the Wadi Al-Salaam Cemetery located in Iraq. It's two miles (six kilometers) squared and it's so big that it's unknown how many bodies are in there. It's estimated to be in the millions and half a million more get added each year.

373. There's a natural gas vent in Iraq known as the Eternal Fire that's been burning for over 4,000 years.

374. There is a city being created in the Arab Emirates right now that will be entirely reliant on renewable energy sources with a zero waste ecology.

375. Ethiopia is currently in the year 2006 because there are thirteen months in its year.

376. The City of New York paid $5 million in 1853 for the land that is Central Park, which is now worth $530 billion.

377. For years, an Indian man named Rajesh Kumar Sharma has been teaching slum children who live under a local metro bridge. Five days a week for two hours a day, he leaves his job at the general store to teach over 140 kids who would otherwise not be able to learn.

378. The pollution in Beijing is so bad they have come up with a term called the "Beijing Cough."

379. Almost a tenth of all Chinese have the last name "Wang" which translates to king.

380. If New York City was its own country and the NYPD was its army, it would be the 20th best funded army in the world just behind Greece and ahead of North Korea.

381. In North Korea, it is currently the year 109 because their calendar is based on the birth of Kim Il-Sung, the founder of North Korea.

382. There are still thirty million people living in caves in China.

383. The Vatican City is home to the world's only ATM that gives instructions in Latin.

384. France was the first country to introduce the registration plate on August 14, 1893.

385. The biggest island in the world is Greenland as Australia is a continent.

386. China produces the most pollution in the world contributing 30% of all the countries total. These come from coal, oil, and natural gases.

387. The most visited city in the world is Bangkok, with twenty million people in 2018, followed by London and Paris.

388. The smallest country in the world is the Vatican which only has 0.22 square miles (0.44 square kilometers).

389. As of 2019, the country with the highest homicide rates is El Salvador with 82.84 homicides per 100,000 inhabitants per year, with a population of approximately six million people that equates to 5,000 people per year. The extremely high homicide rate in this country is marked by significant occurrence of gang-related crimes and juvenile delinquency.

390. "Fancy riding" on bikes is illegal in Illinois. That includes riding without hands or taking your feet off the pedals when you're on the street.

391. There are five countries in the world that don't have airports: Vatican City, San Marino, Monaco, Liechtenstein, and Andorra.

392. Nebraska's official state slogan is "Nebraska: Honestly, it's not for everyone."

393. The entire European Union is smaller than Canada alone. In fact, Canada is thirty three times bigger than Italy and fifteen times bigger than France.

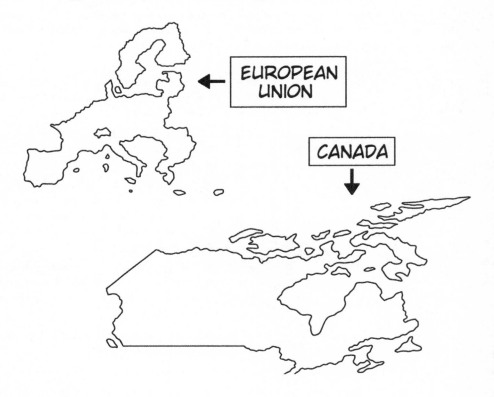

Crimes, Drugs & Prison

394. In 1988, a woman named Jean Terese Keating disappeared while awaiting trial for drunkenly killing a woman in a car crash. She was arrested fifteen years later after bragging at a bar about having gotten away with the crime.

395. In the 1960's, Alcatraz was the only federal prison at the time to offer hot water showers for its inmates. The logic behind it was that prisoners who were acclimated to hot water would not be able to withstand the freezing waters of the San Francisco Bay during an escape attempt.

396. In the 1980's, the infamous kingpin Pablo Escobar was making so much money off of his drug cartel that he was spending $2,500 ($7,200 in today's money) every single month on rubber bands just to hold all of the cash.

397. During the early 1900's, French gangsters used a weapon called "Apache Revolver" that functioned as a revolver, a knife, and brass knuckles.

398. Colombia's underground drug cartel trades as much as $10 billion each year, more than the country's legal exports.

399. A psychologist named Timothy Leary was sent to jail in 1970 and given a series of tests to determine which jail he should be placed in. Since he designed many of the tests himself, he manipulated his answers so that he would be placed in a low security prison as a gardener and ended up escaping only eight months later.

400. The crime rate in Iceland is so low that the police there don't carry guns.

401. A quarter of the world's prisoners are locked up in the US.

402. In 2013, the Netherlands closed eight prisons due to the lack of criminals.

403. A French woman named Nadine Vaujour was so determined to get her husband out of jail that she learned how to fly a helicopter to get him out. She succeeded in picking him up off the roof, however, she was arrested shortly after.

404. Brazil's prisons offer their prisoners the chance to reduce their prison sentence by up to forty eight days a year for every book they read and write a report on.

405. In Italy, the richest business is the mafia that turns over $178 billion a year, which is 7% of the country's GDP.

406. In 2011, a man named Richard James Verone robbed a bank for $1 so that he could be sent to jail to receive free medical health care.

407. In 2008, it was discovered that a fifty six year old crime reporter named Vlado Taneski, who was reporting on gruesome murders, was the serial killer himself.

408. In 2006, the FBI planted a spy in a southern California mosque and disguised him as a radical Muslim in order to root out potential threats. The plan backfired when Muslims in the mosque ended up reporting him to the FBI for being a potentially dangerous extremist.

409. Many murder cases in Japan are declared suicides in order for police officers to save face and to keep crime statistics low.

410. In 1991, there was uncontrolled flooding that caused The Oceanos, a cruise ship, to start to sink. The captain and crew abandoned the ship first, leaving passengers on board without sounding the alarm. Moss Hills, an entertainer aboard the ship, used the radio to call mayday, and everyone was saved. The crew were charged with negligence.

Entertainment Industry

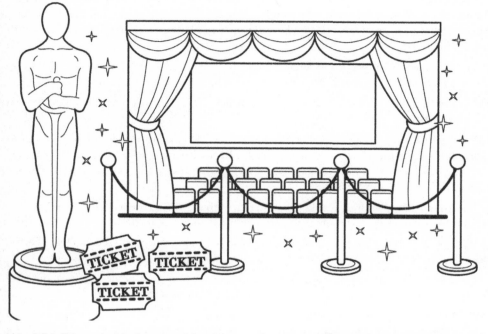

411. Walt Disney holds the record for the most Oscars won by any one person with a total of twenty two.

412. Steven Spielberg waited over ten years after being given the story of the Schindler's List to make the film, as he felt he wasn't mature enough to take on the subject.

413. The mother of Matt Groening, the creator of "The Simpsons," was named Marge Wiggum.

414. The song "Happy Birthday" is 120 years old and has a copyright to it. It's owned by Warner Chappell Music who insists that no one uses it; this is the reason you rarely hear it on TV shows or movies.

415. Bob Marley's last words to his son were: "Money can't buy you life."

416. Nemo makes an appearance in the movie "Monsters Inc." as a toy that Boo gives to Sully a full two years before the movie "Finding Nemo" came out. Pixar movies are infamous for being full of Easter eggs like this.

417. Justin Timberlake's mother was Ryan Gosling's legal guardian when he was a child.

418. Macklemore once worked at a juvenile detention center to help detainees express themselves by writing and creating rap lyrics.

419. Johnny Depp has a passion for playing guitar, playing with artists such as Marilyn Manson, Oasis, Aerosmith, and Eddie Vedder.

420. Lady Gaga stars in the Guinness World Records twelve times. One of them is for including the most product placements in a video.

421. Only a third of the snakes you see in the movie "Snakes on a Plane" were real.

422. In 2007, Joshua Bell, an award winning violinist and conductor, conducted an experiment where he pretended to be a street violinist and had over a thousand people pass him without stopping. He only collected $31 that day yet two days previously sold out to a theater where each seat cost $100. The violin he was playing with on the street was worth $3.5 million.

423. The Lion King was considered a small B movie during productions as all the top Disney animators were working on Pocahontas, which they considered an A movie.

424. Brad Pitt was banned from China for twenty years after his role in the film "Seven Years in Tibet."

425. Reed Hastings, the founder of Netflix, got the idea to start the site when he received a late fine of $40 on a VHS copy of Apollo 13. Reed also approached Blockbuster in 2005 offering to sell the company for $50 million which was turned down at the time. Today the company is worth over $9 billion.

426. Animal Planet aired a fake documentary about the existence of mermaids that convinced thousands of viewers twice, once in 2012 and once in 2013.

427. The American singer and songwriter Dolly Parton once entered a Dolly Parton lookalike contest for fun and ended up losing to a drag queen.

428. The Cookie Monster revealed in 2004 during a song that before he started eating cookies and became known as the "Cookie Monster," he was called "Sid."

429. Lotso, the bear from Toy Story 3, was originally supposed to be in the first movie, but the technology needed to create his fur wasn't available at the time so he got pushed back to the third film.

430. Insurance companies have blacklisted Jackie Chan and anyone else who works on his stunt team. This means that if anyone gets injured while on the set of a Jackie Chan movie, he has to pay for their recovery treatment.

431. National Geographic star Casey Anderson has a pet grizzly bear named Brutus. The bear was adopted in 2002 when he was a newborn cub, and in 2008, served as Casey's best man at his wedding.

432. Before Will Smith starred in the Fresh Prince of Bel-Air, he was on the verge of bankruptcy owing the government $2.8 million. For the first three seasons of the show, he had to pay 70% of his income.

433. Dressed up Disneyland characters never ever break character. They're even given special autograph training sessions so that they can always sign autographs in the style of the cartoon character they're playing.

434. Jim Cummings, the voice of Winnie the Pooh, would call up children's hospitals and talk to them in his Winnie voice to make them feel better.

435. Walt Disney was fired from Kansas City Star in 1919 because his editor said that he lacked imagination and had no good ideas.

436. The person who did the voice of Minnie Mouse, Russi Taylor, was married to Wayne Allowing, the voice of Mickey Mouse.

437. Snoop Dogg has a book published named Rolling Words that has lyrics of all his

songs that you can later rip out and use as rolling papers.

438. There's a restaurant in New Jersey owned by Bon Jovi where there are no fixed prices. Instead customers donate money or volunteer to pay for their meals.

439. Comedian Charlie Chaplan was given an honorary Oscar for his contribution to film in 1972, during the Forty-Fourth annual Academy Awards. During the event, he showed up in the United States after staying away for twenty years because he was labeled a communist. As he went to stage, he was welcomed with a twelve minute standing ovation from the audience and celebrities. This still stands as the longest Oscar in history.

440. In 1961, Mel Blanc, the voice of Bugs Bunny, was in a serious car accident that put him in a coma that he could not wake up from. Doctors began speaking directly to the characters that he voiced from which he would actually respond in their voices, and three weeks later he actually woke up.

441. "Sperm Race" was a show that aired in Germany in 2005 where twelve men donated their sperm to a lab. The doctors then observed the sperm race towards the egg and the winner received a new Porsche.

442. In the early 1990's, Michael Jackson tried to buy Marvel Comics so that he could play Spider Man in his own self-produced movie.

443. In 1939, the New York Times predicted that the television would fail because the average American family wouldn't have enough time to sit around and watch it.

444. If you could actually go to Hogwarts, it would cost approximately $40,000 a year.

445. In the Despicable Me movies, the gibberish that the minions speak is actually a functioning language written by the directors called "Minionese."

446. The original founders and owners of Macy's, Isidor and Ida Straus, both died on the Titanic. They were the old couple in the movie who went to sleep as the ship went down, which is what actually happened.

447. The creator of Peter Pan, J. M. Barrie, gave away the rights of the franchise to the Great Ormond Street Children's Hospital so that they could always collect royalties and fund the hospital.

448. The Prince Charles Cinema in London has volunteer ninjas that sneak up and hush anyone in the theater that's making noise or throwing things.

449. Cameron Diaz and Snoop Dogg both went to school together. Cameron even bought some weed off of Snoop once.

450. An employee at Pixar accidentally deleted a sequence of Toy Story 2 during

production. It would've taken a year to remake what was gone but, luckily, another employee had the whole thing backed up on a personal computer.

451. Space Jam is the highest grossing basketball movie of all time.

452. The Beast from Beauty and the Beast is a creature called a "Chimera" which has features from seven different animals.

453. The entire Pixar staff had to take a graduate class in fish biology before making Finding Nemo.

454. Arnold Schwarzenegger was paid $15 million in the second Terminator film where he only said 700 words of dialogue. At a cost by word basis, his famous line "Hasta la vista baby" cost over $85,000.

455. Twilight was rejected fourteen times before it was accepted.

456. Jackie Chan is an actor as well as a pop star in Asia; he has released twenty albums since 1984. He also sings the theme songs to his own movies.

457. All the characters in Toy Story only blink one eye at a time.

458. It would take over fifty million balloons to lift the average house off the ground like in the movie "Up."

459. In 1938, Walt Disney was awarded an honorary Oscar for Snow White. The statuette that he received came with seven mini-statuettes on a stepped base.

460. Before he was Iron Man, actor Robert Downey Junior was a notorious drug addict. He credits his sobriety to the fast food chain Burger King. In an interview with Empire magazine, he revealed that in 2003 he was driving a car full of drugs when he ordered a burger from Burger King that was so disgusting that he felt compelled to pull over, get out, and dump all of his drugs into the ocean.

461. If you rearrange the first letters of the main character's names in the movie Inception: Dom, Robert, Eames, Arthur, Mal, Saito, they spell "dreams."

462. Verne Troyer, the actor who plays Mini-me in the Austin Powers movies, had to do all his own stunts because at 2.7 feet (eighty one centimeters) tall, there was no stunt double his size that could fill in for him.

463. Bruce Lee's reflexes were so fast that he could snatch a quarter off of a person's open palm and replace it with a penny before the person could close their fist.

464. In the late 1990's, there was a Russian TV show called "The Intercept," where contestants had to steal a car. If they didn't get caught by the police in thirty five minutes, they got to keep the car, otherwise they were arrested.

465. Ryan Gosling was casted for the role of Noah in the movie "The Notebook" because the director wanted someone "not handsome."

466. The actor who plays Mr. Bean, Rowan Atkinson, once saved a plane from crashing after the pilot passed out, despite never having piloted a plane before.

467. There's a movie from 2010 called "Rubber" about a murderous car tire named Robert that rolls around killing people and blowing things up.

468. The average Game of Thrones episode costs $2 to $3 million to produce. That's two to three times what a typical network or cable show costs per episode.

469. Jackie Chan's son will receive none of his $130 million fortune as he's quoted saying: "If he's capable, he can make his own money. If he's not, then he'll just be wasting my money."

470. The monkey in "Hangover 2" is the same one seen in "Night at the Museum." His name is Crystal and he's featured in twenty five other movies as well. He was awarded the Poscar in 2015, which is an Oscar for animals.

471. In 2010, Johnny Depp responded to a letter from a nine year old girl named Beatrice Delap by actually showing up at her school in costume as Captain Jack Sparrow. She wrote asking that pirates help her stage a mutiny against her teachers.

472. Bob Marley was buried with his red Bison guitar, a Bible opened to Psalm 23, and a bud of marijuana.

473. The set used in the 2009 Sherlock Holmes film was reused as the house of Sirius Black in Harry Potter and the Order of the Phoenix.

474. The first ever ticket purchase to the first ever Comic Con in New York was by George R.R. Martin in 1964. He was the first of only thirty people there that day.

475. When Shakira was in the second grade, she was rejected from the school choir because her music teacher didn't think she could sing, and thought she sounded like a goat.

476. Before Scar got the scar on his face in "The Lion King," his name was Taka which means garbage in Swahili.

477. Before Sylvester Stallone sold the script for "Rocky," he was broke and had to sell his dog for $50. A week later he sold the script and bought his dog back for $3,000.

478. Jackie Chan's mother was a drug smuggler while his father was a spy. This is in fact how they met, when his father arrested his mother for smuggling opium.

479. George Lucas wanted the role of Mace Windu to originally go to Tupac, however, he died before he could give an audition and the role went to Samuel L. Jackson instead.

480. Kim Peek, the inspiration for the movie Rain Man, was born with significant brain damage. He's read over 12,000 books and remembers every single one of them. He's even able to read two pages at once, one with each eye.

481. In 2005, a documentary called "Reversal of Fortune" was filmed where film makers gave a homeless man named Ted Rodrigue $100,000 in cash and followed him around to see what he would do with the money. Less than six months later he was completely broke and back in the same place he was before it all started.

482. Oona Chaplin, the actress who plays Talisa in the Game of Thrones, is actually

Charlie Chaplin's granddaughter.

483. Zach Galifianakis was approached by Nike to be in their advertising after the success of The Hangover. During the conference call he broke the ice by asking: "So do you still have seven year olds making your stuff?"

484. When Jackie Chan was eighteen, he got into a street fight with bikers; shortly after he noticed a piece of bone sticking out of his knuckle. He spent an entire day trying to push it back in until he realized that it wasn't his bone but the other guy's tooth.

485. Five hundred stormtroopers were placed on the Great Wall of China by Disney to promote "Star Wars: The Force Awakens."

486. After the movie "Princess and the Frog" came out, more than fifty people were hospitalized with salmonella poisoning from kissing frogs.

487. Irmelin Indenbirken was pregnant and felt her baby kick when she was looking at a Leonardo da Vinci painting in Italy. She ended up naming her son "Leonardo" after the painter, and that's how Leonard DiCaprio got his name.

488. After being eliminated from the show Hell's Kitchen, the contestants are immediately taken to get psychiatric evaluations and then to a house where they are pampered with back rubs, haircuts, and manicures. This is because the experience on the show is so draining that the producers don't want the eliminated contestants to kill themselves or someone else.

489. The first film with a $100 million budget was True Lies, which was made in 1994.

Food & Drinks

490. Colonel Sanders disliked what the KFC Franchise had done to the food so much that he described it as the worst fried chicken he had ever had and that the gravy was like wall paper paste.

491. In 2009, Burger King launched a campaign that if you unfriended ten of your Facebook friends, you would receive a free Whopper. Using the Whopper Sacrifice application, your friend would receive a message telling them that their friendship was less valuable than a Whopper.

492. Potatoes have more chromosomes than a human.

493. Ruth Wakefield, who invented the chocolate chip cookie around 1938, sold the idea to Nestle Toll House in exchange for a lifetime supply of chocolate.

494. Butter milk contains zero butter.

495. The Coca-Cola made in the Maldives used to be made from ocean water.

496. A quarter of the world's hazelnuts each year go towards making Nutella. That's 100,000 tons of hazelnuts per year.

497. Pineapple isn't a fruit, it's actually a berry.

498. France was the first country that banned supermarkets from throwing out or destroying food that wasn't sold.

499. McDonald's has more than 37,000 stores around the world making it the largest fast food chain globally.

500. The pizza Louis XIII is the most expensive pizza in the world costing $12,000. Created by Chef Renato Viola, he prepares the entire dish at your house. The toppings include three types of caviar, Mediterranean lobster, and red prawns. The size of the pizza is only eight inches (twenty centimeters) in diameter.

501. There's a mushroom in the wild called "Laetiporus" that tastes like fried chicken.

502. Black tomatoes can be grown without any genetic engineering. They are full of beneficial anthocyanins which are believed to help with obesity, cancer, and diabetes.

503. In Cambodia, they sell "Happy Pizza" which is a cheese pizza garnished with weed on top.

504. Apples, peaches, and raspberries are all members of the rose family.

505. The average strawberry has 200 seeds on the outside. It's also not considered a fruit.

506. Most of the vitamins you get from eating a potato are in the skin.

507. In 1996, McDonald's opened their first ski-through fast food restaurant in Sweden. People can actually ski up to the counter, order food, and ski off. It is called McSki.

508. Burger King in Japan has released two black hamburgers called the "Kure Diamond" and the "Kuro Pearl" with everything including the bun, the sauce, and the cheese colored black with squid ink.

509. People have been eating potatoes since 7,000 years ago.

510. Coca-Cola was invented by an American pharmacist named John Pemberton who advertised it as a nerve tonic that could cure headaches and fatigue.

511. Half of the DNA in a banana is identical to what makes up you.

512. Roughly a third of all food produced in the world for human consumption every year goes to waste. This is approximately 1.3 billion tons equating to roughly a billion dollars down the drain.

513. In 2014, a competitive eater named Molly Schuyler, who weighs only 126 pounds (fifty seven kilograms), won four eating contests in only three days. She ate a total of 363 chicken wings, fifty nine pancakes, five pounds (2.2 kilograms) of bacon, and five pounds of barbecued meat.

514. In the US, April 2 is National Peanut Butter and Jelly Day.

515. Watermelons contain an ingredient called "citrulline" that can trigger the production of a compound that helps relax the body's blood vessels, just like Viagra.

516. Turophobia is the fear of cheese.

517. Doritos can be made without the powder and taste exactly the same, but the company intentionally adds it because they believe it adds to the Doritos experience.

518. You can make your own Gatorade at home by simply adding salt to some Kool-Aid. It's not the exact recipe, but it's got just as many electrolytes.

519. A tablespoon of cake frosting has less fat, calories, and sugar than a tablespoon of Nutella.

520. "Oriole O's" are a type of cereal that's exclusively available in South Korea.

521. There is a secret McDonald's menu item that you can order which is a McChicken in the middle of a double cheeseburger.

522. Ben and Jerry's has a cemetery where they bury all their discontinued flavors.

523. Skittles and jelly beans contain insect cocoons which are used to coat candies to give them that special shine known as shellac.

524. Coca leaves are still used by Coca-Cola to this day. A company in New Jersey first extracts the cocaine from the leaves giving the spent leaves to Coca-Cola to put in their drinks.

525. In China, it's possible to buy baby pears shaped like Buddha. The farmers actually clamp a mold onto a growing fruit to get the shape. There is also a company called "Fruit Mold" that makes heart-shaped cucumbers, square watermelons, and other more deliciously weird shapes.

526. Before the seventeenth century, carrots were purple until a mutation changed the color to what we know now.

527. Diet soda ruins your tooth enamel just as badly as cocaine and methamphetamines.

528. There is a Pizza Hut perfume that smells like a fresh box of Pizza Hut pizza when you spray it.

529. The creator of Pringles, Fredric Baur, had his ashes stored in a Pringles can after he died.

530. Chewing gum when cutting onions prevents you from tearing up as it forces you to breathe through your mouth.

531. Honey is the only food that doesn't spoil.

532. Coca-Cola only sold twenty five bottles its first year. Today, it sells 1.8 billion bottles a day.

533. There are no genuinely blue foods. Foods that appear blue such as blueberries are often a shade of purple.

534. Marshmallows exist because of sore throats. For centuries, juice from the marshmallow plant has been used for pain relief. In the 1800's, it was mixed with egg whites and sugar for children with sore throats, and the recipe was so tasty that people turned it into a treat

called marshmallow.

535. The stickers that you find on fruit are actually made of edible paper and the glue used to stick them on is actually food grade, so even if you eat one, you'll be completely fine.

536. Cherries contain two compounds inhibiting tumor growth and even cause cancer cells to self-destruct without damaging healthy cells.

537. The artificial sweetener Splenda was discovered when a researcher misheard the command "to test this chemical" as "taste this chemical."

538. Oranges are not even in the top ten list of common foods when it comes to vitamin C levels.

539. The top ten cheese eating countries are all in Europe with France being number one. The average French person consumes fifty seven pounds (twenty five kilograms) of cheese per year.

540. Sugar was first invented in India where extraction and purification techniques were developed in 510 B.C. Before that the most popular sweetener was honey.

541. The typical American spends $1,200 on fast food every year.

542. All of the air in potato chip bags that people complain about isn't air at all. It's actually nitrogen which serves the purpose to keep chips crisp and to provide a cushion during shipping.

543. There's a fruit called "black sapote" or "chocolate pudding fruit" which, at the right ripeness, tastes like chocolate pudding, is low in fat and has about four times as much vitamin C as an orange.

544. One hundred acres of pizza are cut every day in the US alone.

545. In 2013, Scottish scientists created a pizza that has 30% of your daily recommended nutrients.

546. A twenty ounce bottle of Mountain Dew contains the equivalent of twenty two packets of sugar.

547. In France, a bakery by law has to make all its bread that it sells from scratch in order to have the right to be called a bakery.

548. Supermarket apples can be a year old. They're usually picked between August and November, covered in wax, hot-air dried, and sent into cold storage. After six to twelve months, they finally land on the grocery store shelves.

549. In the Philippines, McDonald's includes spaghetti in their menu. The pasta comes with a beef tomato sauce and a piece of "McDo" fried chicken.

550. Cucumber slices can fight bad breath. If you don't have a mint on hand, a slice of cucumber will do the job.

551. More than 1/5 of all the calories consumed by humans worldwide is provided by rice alone.

552. There is a McDonald's in every continent except Antarctica.

553. Even though Froot Loops are different colors, they all have exactly the same flavor.

Funny

554. George Garrett, a nineteen year old man from England, changed his name to "Captain Fantastic Faster Than Superman Batman Wolverine The Hulk And The Flash Combined" in 2008.

555. In 2013, in Belo Horizonte, Brazil, construction workers permanently cemented a truck into a sidewalk after the owner refused to move it.

556. There's a travel agency in Tokyo called "Unagi Travel" that, for a fee, will take your stuffed animal on vacation around the world.

557. There's a museum in Europe called the "Museum of Broken Relationships" that exclusively displays objects that were meaningful to heartbroken exes.

558. The "over 9,000" meme that was popularized from Dragon Ball Z was a translation error. The power level was actually over 8,000.

559. The Curiosity Rover sang Happy Birthday to itself on Mars to commemorate the one year anniversary of landing on the planet in 2013.

560. "Backpfeifengesicht" is a German word that means a face that badly needs a punch.

561. If police in Thailand misbehave, they're punished by being made to wear bright pink Hello Kitty armbands.

562. Due to the aging population in Japan, adult diaper sales are about to surpass baby diaper sales.

563. The Vystavochnaya subway station in Moscow accepts thirty squats as payment for a metro ticket as an incentive to exercise more.

564. In the Victorian era, special tea cups that protected your mustache from getting dunked in your tea were used.

565. Disneyland does not sell any gum. This is because Walt Disney didn't want people stepping in gum as they walked around the park.

566. In 2008, The North Face clothing company sued a clothing company called "The South Butt."

567. The earliest "your momma joke" was written on a tablet 3,500 years ago by a student in Ancient Babylon.

568. Bangkok University in Thailand makes their students wear anti-cheating helmets during exams.

569. There's a lake in Australia called "Lake Disappointment" that was named and found by Frank Hann in 1897, who was hoping to find fresh water but instead found salt water.

570. International "have a bad day" day is November 19th.

571. The traffic in London is as slow as the carriages from a century ago.

572. Before alarm clocks were invented, there was a profession called a "knocker up" which involved going from client to client and tapping on their windows or banging on their doors with long sticks until they were awake. This lasted till the 1920's.

573. There is a town in Alaska called "Talkeetna" that has had a cat named Stubbs as its honorary mayor since 1997.

574. Putting dry tea bags in smelly shoes or gym bags is an easy and quick way to absorb any unpleasant odors.

575. From the poll of 2,500 participants, the average person spends forty two minutes a week or almost ninety two days over a lifetime on the toilet.

576. The founders Bill Hewlett and David Packard flipped a coin to decide whether the company they created would be called "Hewlett-Packard" (HP) or "Packard-Hewlett" (PH).

577. In 1860, Abraham Lincoln grew his famous beard because he got a letter from an eleven year old girl named Grace Bedell who said that all ladies liked the whiskers and they would convince their husbands to vote for him for president.

578. Donald Duck comics were banned from Finland because he isn't wearing any pants.

579. The first ever modern toilet was created by Thomas Crapper, hence the phrase "to take a crap."

580. According to an analysis conducted by Swift Key, Canada uses the poop emoji more than any other country in the world. In France hearts are number one, while Australia leads the world in alcohol and drug related emojis.

581. There are gold glitter pills you can buy for $400 online that promise to turn your poop gold.

582. On Valentine's Day 2014, a group of single men in Shanghai bought every odd-numbered seat for a theater showing of Beijing Love Story. They did this to prevent couples from sitting together as a show of support for single people.

583. In 2014, the Department of Transportation in Colorado was forced to change their mile marker from 420 to 419.99 just to get people to stop stealing their sign.

584. In North Korea, citizens are forced to choose from one of the twenty eight government approved haircuts.

585. In 2005, a man named Ronald McDonald robbed a Wendy's in Manchester, England.

586. In 2013, a fifty nine year old man named Alan Markovitz was upset at his ex-wife for cheating on him, bought a house next to hers, and installed a giant $7,000 statue of a hand giving the finger aimed at her house.

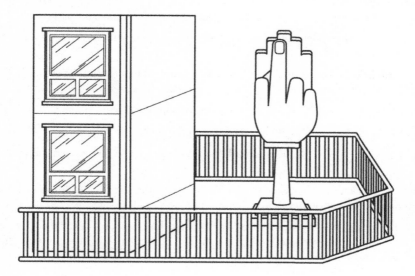

History & Culture

587. The modern handshake dates all the way back to the 5th century B.C., where swordsmen would greet each other with their weapon hand free, showing no sign of a fight.

588. The unbroken seal on Tutankhamun's tomb went untouched for 3,245 years until 1942.

589. An ancient Persian poet recorded the fable of a king that challenged wise men to make him a ring that made him happy when he was sad and sad when he was happy. They succeeded by giving him a ring etched with the phrase: "This too shall pass."

590. Ancient Roman charioteers earned more money than what international sports stars get paid today.

591. One of the clauses in the 1781 US Articles of Confederation states that if Canada wants to be admitted into the US, it'll be automatically accepted.

592. Ancient Rome was eight times more densely populated than modern New York.

593. In Victorian London, mail used to be delivered twelve times per day.

594. The Appian Way in Rome is a road that was built in 312 B.C. that is still used to this day.

595. The largest empire the world has ever seen was the British Empire which covered almost a quarter of the planet in its peak in 1920.

596. In ancient Athens, the world's first democracy, they had a process called "ostracism" where, once a year, the people could vote on the politician that they felt was the most destructive to the democratic process and that person was banished from Athens for ten

years.

597. The Vikings used to find new lands by releasing ravens from their boats and following where they went. They became their favorite symbol and resulted in them using the bird on their flag.

598. Cats used to be sacred in Egypt; if you killed one, you could be sentenced to death. The Egyptians would even shave off their eyebrows to show grief from the death of their cat.

599. The richest man in history was Emperor Mansa Musa's whose wealth is believed to have been around $400 billion when taking into account inflation.

600. In the ancient Persian Empire, men used to debate ideas twice, once sober and once drunk, as they believed an idea had to sound good in both states in order to be considered a good idea.

601. There is a tribe in India called the "War Khasi" that has been passing down for generations the art of manipulating tree roots to create a system of living bridges.

602. Woman have been using pregnancy tests since 1350 B.C. They used to pee on wheat and barley seeds to determine if they were pregnant or not. If wheat grew, it predicted a female baby; and if barley grew, it predicted a male. The woman was not pregnant if nothing grew. This theory was tested and proved accurate 70% of the time.

603. Democracy was invented in Greece 2,500 years ago.

604. Romans used urine to clean and whiten their teeth. They were actually onto something as urine contains ammonia which has a cleaning substance that results into clearing out everything.

605. During the 1600's, there was "Tulip Mania" in Holland where tulips were more valuable than gold. This is the first reported economic bubble. When people came to their senses, the bubble burst and caused the market to crash.

606. In the early 1930's, a social movement became popular although it eventually died out, which proposed replacing politicians and business people with scientists and engineers that could manage the economy.

607. There are still several unexplored hidden passages in the pyramids of Giza.

608. Teddy Roosevelt was shot in 1912 right before giving a speech. Noticing that it missed his lungs, since he wasn't coughing up blood, he proceeded to give the full ninety minute speech.

609. Socialist Karl Marx's final words before he died in 1883 were: "Go away, last words are for fools who haven't said enough."

610. The popular saying "bless you" after a sneeze originated from the 14th century, when Pope Gregory the VII asked for it to be said after every time he sneezed so he could be

protected against the plague.

611. The shortest presidency in the history of the world was by President Pedro Paredes of Mexico, who ruled for less than one hour on February 19, 1913.

612. Ancient Egyptians used headrests made of stone instead of pillows.

613. There are 350 pyramids that were built by the rulers of the ancient Kushite kingdoms now known as Sudan.

614. In 2013, a lost Egyptian city named Heracleion was discovered underwater after being lost for 1,200 years in the Mediterranean Sea.

615. In 1770, the British Parliament passed a law condemning lipstick, stating that any woman found guilty of seducing a man into matrimony by a cosmetic means would be tried for witchcraft.

616. A "butt" was a medieval unit of measurement for wine. Technically, a butt-load of wine is 125 gallons (475 liters).

617. The first ever diamonds were found in India in the 4th century B.C. The next country it was discovered in was Brazil in 1725.

618. In Japanese myth, there's a creature called "Asiarai Yashiki." It's a giant unwashed foot that appears before you and demands to be washed. If you don't wash it, it rampages through your house.

619. The oldest instruments date back 43,000 years ago, which were flutes made out of bones from birds and mammoths.

Human Body & Human Behavior

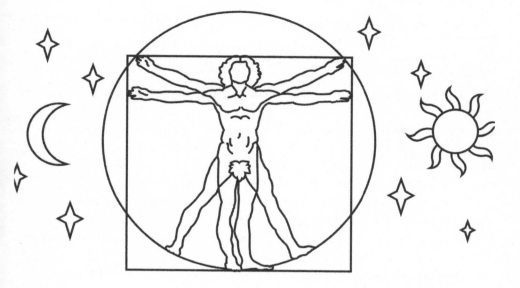

620. If an astronaut got out of his space suit on the moon, he would explode before he suffocated.

621. There are tiny eight legged creatures that are closely related to spiders living in the pores of your facial skin; they are called "demodex."

622. Contrary to popular belief, white spots on fingernails are not a sign of a deficiency of calcium, zinc, or other vitamins in the diet. They're actually called "leukonychia," are completely harmless, and are most commonly caused by minor injuries that occur while the nail is growing.

623. Mobile phones emit electro-magnetic frequencies that heat body tissue and can affect over a hundred proteins in the brain.

624. Ischaemic heart disease and stroke are the world's biggest killers. Ischaemic means an inadequate blood supply to an organ.

625. The average person will fall asleep in just seven minutes.

626. You would be a few centimeters taller in space due to the lack of gravity there.

627. If you were to take out someone's lung and flatten it out, it would have the same surface area as one half of a tennis court.

628. There is enough carbon in your body to make over 9,000 pencils.

629. The hippocampus, which is responsible for memory, is larger in women's brains than in men's.

630. Humans have twenty three pairs of chromosomes while great apes have twenty four.

631. As a person dies, his or her hearing is the last sense to go.

632. The human brain can compute over a thousand processes per second, making it quicker than any computer.

633. The sound you hear when you put a seashell next to your ear isn't the sea but your blood running through your veins.

634. The information travelling inside your brain is moving at 268 miles per hour (430 kilometers per hour).

635. There are only two parts on the human body that never stop growing, the ears and the nose.

636. There's a phobia called the "Jonah complex" which causes a person to fear their own success, preventing them from reaching their full potential.

637. There is a condition called "hyperthymesia" that causes the person to remember every single detail of their lives. Only twelve people on earth have this condition.

638. Although the brain is physically developed by the age of five, the rational part of a brain isn't fully developed and won't be until age twenty five.

639. The average adult has eight pounds (3.6 kilograms) or about twenty two square feet (two square meters) of skin.

640. Humans are capable of feeling the effects of a broken heart. This is known as "stress cardiomyopathy" in medical terms. If you're suffering from a broken heart, your blood can have three times the amount of adrenaline than someone suffering from a heart attack.

641. Even after six hours of being dead, a person's muscles continue to spasm periodically.

642. We miss 10% of everything we see due to blinking.

643. There are 1,000 gigabytes in a terabyte and most neuroscientists estimate that the human brain can hold between ten and 100 terabytes of information.

644. There is a side effect of sleep deprivation called "microsleep" in which a person will fall asleep for a few seconds or even a few minutes without realizing it. It's extremely dangerous and is one of the largest contributors to accidents on the road.

645. There's a syndrome called "Tetris Effect" that occurs when people dedicate so much time and attention to an activity that it starts to pattern their thoughts, mental images, and dreams.

646. A study conducted by Loma Linda University in 2010 concluded that laughter not only reduces stress, but it increases the production of antibodies and kills the activity of tumor cells.

647. Crying is actually very healthy for you. It helps you emotionally, lubricates your eyes, removes toxins and irritants, and reduces stress.

648. According to a study done by Mekuin University in Canada, playing video games before bedtime actually gives a person the ability to control their dreams. It also suggests that gamers are more likely to have lucid dreams as opposed to non-gamers.

649. The offspring of two identical sets of twins are legally cousins but genetically siblings.

650. Atelophobia is the fear of not being good enough or having imperfections.

651. All humans have lines on our bodies called "Blaschko's lines" which can only be seen under certain conditions such as UV light.

652. Dyslexic people actually see numbers and letters backwards. It's basically a reading disorder, not a vision or seeing disorder. This means that Braille readers can also be dyslexic.

653. The human hearing range is from twenty to 20,000 hertz. If it was any lower than twenty, we'd be able to hear our muscles move.

654. Contrary to popular belief, washing your hands in warm water doesn't kill any more bacteria than washing them in cold water. This is because bacteria only die when water is boiling.

655. The nose is connected to the memory center of your brain, hence why smell triggers some of the most powerful memories.

656. Climonia is the excessive desire to stay in bed all day.

657. Blind people who have never seen before will still smile despite never having seen anyone else do it before because it's a natural human reaction.

658. Veronica Seider holds the Guinness World Record for the best sight in the world. She can see twenty times better than the average person, being able to identify someone's face from one mile (1.6 kilometers) away.

659. If your eye were a digital camera, it would have 576 megapixels in them.

660. Contrary to popular belief, cracking your bones doesn't hurt your bones or cause you arthritis. It's simply the gas bubbles bursting that you hear; however, doing it too much does cause tissue damage.

661. When a person lies, they experience an increase in temperature around the nose known as the Pinocchio effect.

662. There are actually seven different types of twins. They are: identical, fraternal, half-identical, mirror image, mixed chromosome, superfetation, and superfecundation.

663. Adding sugar to a wound will greatly reduce the pain and speed up the healing process.

664. Only 1 to 2% of the total world population are redheads.

665. Like fingerprints, our tongues all have unique prints.

666. You are born with 270 bones which form into 206 by the time you're an adult. A quarter of these are in your hands and wrists.

667. During the lifespan of a human, enough saliva can be created to fill up two swimming pools.

668. Humans can only live without oxygen for three minutes, water for three days, and food for three weeks.

669. The length of human vessels in the body equate to 60,000 miles (96,000 kilometers) if you lay them out from beginning to end.

670. Smokers are four times more likely to get grey hair in their lives than non-smokers.

671. All humans have the ability to see ultraviolet light, however, it's passively filtered through our lens. People who get surgery done to remove the lens are then able to see ultraviolet light.

672. Farting helps to reduce blood pressure and is good for overall health.

673. Studies have been shown that people with creative minds find it harder to fall asleep at night and prefer to stay up later.

674. It was discovered that people are most likely to have a good idea when they're doing a monotonous task such as showering, driving, or exercising. This is due to the fact that the body is in a more relaxed and less distracted state, allowing dopamine to flow through the body, triggering thoughts.

675. Patients in an insane mental asylum in the 1950's have the same stress as the average high school student nowadays.

676. Humans take in eleven million bits of information every second, however, we're only aware of about forty of these things.

677. 95% of the decisions you make have already been made up by your subconscious mind.

678. By the time you are two, your brain is already 80% the size of an adult's.

679. The average person has 10,000 taste buds which are replaced every two weeks.

680. Humans can have anywhere from twelve to sixty thousand thoughts per day with 80% of these thoughts being negative.

681. The human brain has 100 billion brain cells.

682. Each sperm contains about three billion bases of genetic information, representing 750 megabytes of digital information.

683. It's impossible to taste food without saliva. This is because chemicals from the food must first dissolve in saliva. Once dissolved, chemicals can be detected by receptors on taste buds.

684. Astronauts would weigh one sixth of their weight if they were in space compared to

on Earth.

685. You cannot invent faces in your dreams, which means you've encountered every face you've seen in real life.

686. The human eye can see a candle flickering up to thirty miles (forty eight kilometers) away on a dark night.

687. Due to a genetic mutation, the first blue eyed humans only began to appear six to ten thousand years ago.

688. The act of "fubbing" or "phone snubbing" is becoming a very real epidemic among Americans according to new research published in the Journal of Computers and Human Behavior. Fubbing is the act of snubbing someone in a social situation by looking down at the phone instead of paying attention to them; this behavior can affect and damage relationships, even leading to severe depression and lower rates of life satisfaction.

689. If you don't identify yourself as an extrovert or introvert, you may be an ambivert, which is a person moderately comfortable with groups and social interactions, but who also relishes time alone away from crowds.

690. We're technically living about eighty milliseconds in the past because that's how long it takes our brain to process information.

691. The human brain has a negativity bias causing us to continually look for bad news. It's an evolutionary trait that stem from early humans as a survival mechanism.

692. Only 2% of the Earth's population has green eyes.

693. Being hungry causes serotonin levels to drop, causing a whirlwind of uncontrollable emotions including anxiety, stress, and anger.

694. When you're buried six feet down in soil and without a coffin, an average adult body normally takes eight to twelve years to decompose to a skeleton.

695. The largest organ on the body is the skin.

696. The human brain uses 20% of the body's energy even though it's only 2% of the body's total weight.

697. The Neanderthal's brain was 10% bigger than ours, the homosapiens, but they were not as intellectual as us. This is because their brains were more devoted to vision while ours is devoted to reasoning, decision making, and social interaction.

698. The human body contains trillions of microorganisms like bacteria, outnumbering human cells by ten to one.

699. People can have a psychological disorder called boanthropy that makes them believe that they are a cow. They try to live their life as a cow.

Interesting

700. Barcode scanners actually read the spaces between the black bars, not the black bars themselves.

701. There's a religion called "Christian Atheism" where practitioners believe in essentially the same things as traditional Christians, except that the Bible is completely metaphorical and that God is an allegory for human morality rather than a real being.

702. A can of regular coke will sink to the bottom of water while a can of diet coke will float.

703. In 1976, an underachieving Princeton student named John Aristotle Phillips wrote a term paper describing how to build a nuclear bomb. He received an "A," but never got his paper back as it was seized by the FBI.

704. Coal power stations put out 100 times more radiation into the air than nuclear power plants producing the same amount of energy.

705. Percussive maintenance is the technical term for hitting something until it works.

706. There are no clocks in the casinos of Las Vegas so customers lose track of time and stay in the premises longer.

707. When you get blackout drunk, you don't actually forget anything because your brain wasn't recording in the first place.

708. Labeorphilist is the collection and study of beer bottle labels.

709. Popes can't be organ donors because their entire body has to be buried intact as it belongs to the universal Catholic Church.

710. There used to be sheep that grazed in Central Park up until 1934. They were moved during the Great Depression as it was feared they'd be eaten.

711. Halieutics is the study of fishing.

712. The Titanic used to have its own newspaper called "The Atlantic Daily Bulletin." It was printed daily on board and it had news, ads, stock prices, horse racing results, gossip, and the day's menu.

713. It is estimated that only 8% of the world's total money is real. The rest exists electronically on computer hard drives and bank accounts.

714. Over 50% of all lottery tickets sold are bought by only 5% of people who buy lottery tickets.

715. A study conducted by the University of Oxford found that for every person that you fall in love with and accommodate into your life, you lose two close friends.

716. If you open your eyes in a pitch-black room, the color you'll see is called "eigengrau."

717. The Pentagon spends over $250,000 each year to study the body language of world leaders like Vladimir Putin.

718. Studies have shown that smoking hookah is no safer than smoking cigarettes and, in fact, may cause the smoker to absorb more toxic substances than cigarettes.

719. The youngest pope to ever be elected was Pope Benedict IX, born in 1012, who was only twelve years old.

720. In 2000, the KKK adopted a stretch of highway near St. Louis so the Missouri government responded by renaming the road Rosa Parks Highway.

721. Triskaidekaphobia is the fear of the number 13.

722. Stalin's guards were so afraid of him that no one called a doctor for over ten hours after he had a stroke resulting in his death. They feared that he might recover and execute anyone who acted outside of his orders.

723. Eccrinology is the study of excretion.

724. There is a condition called "math anxiety" which causes people to perform poorly in mathematics, not because they're ungifted in math, but because the condition causes their brain to enter such a state where they simply cannot perform math.

725. Oikology is the science of housekeeping.

726. A man named Jonathan Lee Riches got in the Guinness Book of World Records for

having filed the highest number of lawsuits in the world with a total of over 2,600.

727. A stock exchange system exists with pirates in Somalia. Locals can invest in a pirate group and, after a successful heist, they will receive a reward. In one instance a woman gave an RPG 7 to a pirate group and ended up receiving $75,000.

728. Papaphobia is the fear of the pope.

729. A false awakening is the term used for a vivid or convincing dream about awakening from sleep when in reality you're still sleeping.

730. One lightning bolt has enough energy to toast one hundred thousand slices of bread.

731. Reciprocal liking is a psychological term used to describe when you start liking someone after you find out that they like you. It's a phenomenon that reflects the way people feel better about themselves and enjoy the company of those that provide them with positive feelings.

732. Sternutaphobia is the fear of sneezing.

733. The chances of an American being killed by lightning is the same chance a person in Japan has being shot and killed by a gun.

734. A study done in 1915 by the Chicago University concluded that the easiest color to see from a distance was the color yellow, hence the most popular taxi color.

735. Chaology is the study of chaos or chaos theory.

736. Getting hit by lightning heats up your skin to 50,000 degrees Fahrenheit (27,000 degrees Celsius), which is hotter than the surface of the Sun.

737. There is term known as "friend paradox" where the average person has less friends than his friend.

738. The Bingham Canyon Copper Mine in Utah is the largest man made hole at half a mile (one kilometer) deep and two miles (four kilometers) wide; it covers 770 hectares.

739. Deltiology is the collection and study of picture postcards.

740. Cherophobia is the fear of being happy or joyful with the expectation that something bad will happen.

741. The reason a whip creates a whipping sound is because it's moving quicker than the speed of sound creating a small sonic boom.

742. It is estimated that about 100 billion people have died since Homo sapiens appeared over 200,000 years ago.

743. The world's largest gold bar is 551 pounds (250 kilograms).

744. In 1979, debris from NASA's Space Station Skylab crash landed in the town of Esperance, Western Australia, for which the town fined NASA $400 for littering. They actually paid it.

745. Many animal shelters will not allow black cats to be adopted around Halloween time because most people just buy them as impulse purchases.

746. The fear of clowns is called "coulrophobia."

747. In 2011, Lego produced 381 million tires, making them the world's largest rubber tire manufacturer by number of units produced.

748. If you went through seventeen tons of gold ore and one ton of personal computers, you'd find more gold from the personal computers.

749. Two thousand five hundred and twenty is the smallest number that can be divided by all numbers between one and ten.

750. Back in the day, when rabbit ears were put behind a man's head, it meant that his wife was cheating on him. The two fingers held up symbolized the horns of a stag, which had apparently lost its mate to a rival stag.

751. More than half of the world's population is under the age of thirty.

752. According to a study conducted by Brock University in Ontario, Canada, racism and homophobia are linked to having lower IQ, as those with lower intelligence tend to gravitate toward socially conservative ideologies.

753. Anuptaphobia is the fear of either remaining unmarried or marrying the wrong person.

754. The Kuwaiti Dinar is the strongest currency in the world with one Dinar equating to $3.29 USD.

755. Pirates used to wear eye patches on one eye during the day so they could see better at night with that same eye.

756. Big Ben in London is not the tower but the bell inside.

757. A bus can replace forty cars if people made the switch.

758. Diamonds are actually not that rare. A company called "De Beers" owns 95% of the market and suppresses supply to keep the prices high.

759. Campanology is the art of bell ringing.

760. The clothing store H&M stands for Hennes & Mauritz.

761. The pinky swear came from Japan and indicated that if someone broke the promise, they must cut off their pinky.

762. Trypophobia is the fear of holes.

763. The reason people traditionally put wedding rings on the left ring finger is because before medical science figured out how the circulatory system functioned, people believed that there was a vein that ran directly from the fourth finger of the left hand to the heart.

764. Anything that melts can be made into glass, however, there will be molten residue stuck to it.

765. The nicotine from one puff of a cigarette reaches your brain in seven seconds. Alcohol take approximately six minutes.

766. Antibiotics are actually ineffective against fighting viruses. They are only effective against bacterial infections.

767. Oil expands with the rise of temperature, hence if you're filling your car up, it's best in the morning or late at night when it's not hot to get the most bang for your buck.

768. The World Health Organization states that from the one billion smokers in the world more than 600,000 people die every year from secondhand smoke.

769. Until the 1930's, the letter "E" was used to represent a failing grade in the US, however, that was changed to "F" as professors began to worry that their students would mistake "E" for excellent.

770. The term for forgetting something after walking through a doorway is called an "event boundary."

771. Using a paper towel after washing your hands decrease bacteria by 40% while using an air dryer increases the bacteria by up to 220%, as bacteria grow quickly in warm and moist environments.

772. The word font only refers to things like italics, size, and boldness. The style of the lettering is called a "typeface."

773. If the 1st of January on a leap year falls on a Sunday, the months of January, April, and July will each have a Friday 13th. In the 20th century, this happened in 1928, 1956, and 1984. In the 21st century, this will happen four times in 2012, 2040, 2068, and 2096.

774. The average IQ rate has been declining over recent decades. This is because smarter people are having less children.

775. Brass door knobs automatically disinfect themselves in eight hours, which is known as the "oligodynamic effect."

776. Schools that ditch schoolyard rules are actually seeing a decrease in bullying, serious injuries, and vandalism, while concentration levels in class are increasing. This is because fewer rules requires critical thinking whereas simply obeying instructions requires very little critical thinking.

777. A study conducted in 2011 by Angela Duckworth proved that IQ tests can be affected by motivation. By promising subjects monetary rewards, she found that the higher the reward, the higher they scored on the IQ test.

778. There's only one Shell gas station shaped like a shell. Eight were built in the 1930's, but the only one left is in North Carolina.

779. You can see four states from the top of Chicago's Willis Tower on a clear day; it's about forty to fifty miles away, beyond Illinois and out to Indiana, Michigan, and Wisconsin.

780. The collars on men's dress shirts used to be detachable. This was to save on laundry costs as the collar was the part that needed cleaning the most frequently.

781. The first roller coaster was used to transport coal down a hill. After people found that it could reach speeds of up to fifty miles per hour, tourists asked to ride on it for a few cents.

Inventions & Inventors

$$\mathcal{E} = mc^2$$

$$mu\ du\ u\ dm = x\ dm \quad z$$

$$w = \frac{m\ e\ V_0}{2} + a$$

$$f = d\ (mu) / dt$$

$$c^2 - m^2 u^2 = mo^2 c^2$$

782. The Gatling gun was invented by Doctor Richard Gatling, who noticed that the majority of soldiers during the Civil War who died were due to disease, not gunshot wounds. By inventing a machine that could replace hundreds of soldiers, the need for large armies would be reduced thus diminishing exposure to battle and disease.

783. The first hard drive was invented in 1956 and weighed over a ton.

784. Thomas Edison taught his second wife, Mina Miller, Morse code so that they could communicate in secret by tapping each other's hands when their families were around.

785. Inventor Nikola Tesla and author Mark Twain were best friends and were mutual fans of each other's work.

786. The man who designed Saddam Hussein's secret bunker was the grandson of the woman who designed Adolf Hitler's.

787. Manel Torres, a Spanish fashion designer, invented the world's first spray on clothing which can be worn, washed, and worn again.

788. In 1949, the Prince motor company in Japan developed an electric car that could travel 124 miles (200 kilometers) on a single charge.

789. The "Pythagorean cup," also known as a "Greedy cup," is a cup designed to spill its content if too much wine is poured in, encouraging moderation.

790. When dying in 1955, Einstein refused surgery saying: "I want to go when I want, it's tasteless to prolong life artificially, I've done my share, it's time to go, I will do it elegantly."

791. As of 2019, the largest yacht in the world named Azzam is 590 feet long (the length of two football fields) and cost $600 million to build. It was created in 2013, taking four years to construct and beat the previous world record by a full fifty seven feet. It has 94,000 horsepower and can go up to thirty seven miles (sixty kilometers) per hour, the fastest speed for a yacht longer than 300 feet (ninety one meters).

792. The electric chair to execute people was created by a dentist.

793. Bluetooth got its name from Ericsson's Viking Heritage, the Swedish communication company. It's named after Danish Viking King Harold Blatand. Blatand translates to Bluetooth in English and incredibly the Bluetooth symbol is actually Blatand's initials inscribed in runic symbols.

794. In 2004, Volvo introduced a concept car called "YYC" that was built specifically for women without a hood and dent resistant bumpers.

795. Created in Germany, ESSLack is the world's first edible spray paint that comes in gold, silver, red, and blue.

796. There is a device known as "ventricular assist" device or VAD that can permanently replace the function of your heart. The only side effect is you have no pulse.

797. There are now digital pens that can record everything you write, draw or sketch on any surface.

798. Scientists from ATR Computational Neuroscience Laboratories in Tokyo, Japan, have successfully developed a technology that can put thoughts on a computer screen.

799. When tractor owner Ferruccio Lamborghini voiced his frustration over his clutch in the Ferrari to car's founder Enzo Ferrari, Enzo insulted him telling him that the problem was with the driver, not the car. Ferruccio decided to start his own car company and thus the Lamborghini was born.

800. In 1936, the Russians created a computer that ran on water.

801. Bubble wrap was originally invented in 1957 to be sold as wallpaper.

802. The Kevlar bulletproof vest was invented by a pizza delivery guy after being shot twice on the job.

803. The tin can was invented in 1810. The can opener was invented forty eight years later. People used hammers and chisels between this time.

804. The Centennial Light Bulb in Livermore, California, has been burning since 1901 and is the world's longest lasting light bulb according to the Guinness Book of World Records. The bulb is at least 113 years old and has only been turned off a handful of times.

805. It took a whole month for Erno Rubik, the inventor of the Rubik's cube, to solve his own creation.

806. In the summer of 1932, while sitting in a restaurant, Adolf Hitler designed the prototype for what would become the first Volkswagen Beetle.

807. Volvo invented the three point seat belt, but opened up the patent to any car manufacturer who wanted to use it, as they felt it had more value as a lifesaving tool than something to profit from.

808. There's a company called "True Mirror" that makes non reversing mirrors that show you how you actually appear to other people.

809. There's a company named Neurowear that sells a headphone that can read your brainwaves and selects music based on your state of mind.

810. In 2007, a man named Mike Warren-Madden designed a device called the "Aquatic Pram" that allows you to take your fish for a walk.

811. The lighter was invented before the matchstick.

812. Otto Fredrick Rohwedder was the first person to sell sliced bread, and he did it in America in 1928, in Davenport, Iowa. In 1912, Otto invented the single loaf bread slicing machine, which was the first in the world. He marketed his invention as the single greatest advancement in the baking industry, since they started wrapping bread, and he was right, because we term great ideas these days as "the greatest thing since sliced bread."

Kids

813. Some estimates report that one in eight babies is given to the wrong parents at some point during their hospital stay.

814. In Armenia, all children age six and up are taught chess in school as a mandatory part of their curriculum.

815. In Iceland, it's forbidden to give your child a name that hasn't been approved by the Icelandic naming committee.

816. In 2013, France banned child beauty pageants because they promote the hypersexualization of minors. Anyone who organizes such a pageant could face jail time for up to two years and a fine of up to 30,000 euros.

817. A seven year old second grader was suspended for biting a pop tart into the shape of a mountain which school officials mistook for a gun.

818. The reason Lego heads have holes in them is so air can pass through them if a child ever swallows one.

819. In Quebec, Sweden, and Norway, it's illegal to advertise directly to children. This is to prevent companies from encouraging children to beg their parents to buy them stuff.

820. A study done by the Bureau of Economic Research concluded that first born children have higher IQs than their younger siblings.

821. In a study to improve hospital design for children, researchers from the University of Sheffield polled 250 children regarding their opinions of clowns. Every single one reported disliking or fearing them.

Languages

822. Coffee was so influential in early Turkish culture that the word for "breakfast" literally translates to "before coffee," and the word "brown translates" to "the color of coffee."

823. German used to be the second most widely spoken language in the United States before it was forcibly repressed during World War One.

824. "Almost" is the longest English word in alphabetical order.

825. The Hawaiian alphabet only has twelve letters. They are a, e, i, o, u, h, k, l, m, n, p, and w.

826. The English word orange was the name of the fruit for a few hundred years before the color was later named after the fruit. Before that what we now know as orange was known as yee-o-ler-eed.

827. Since the beginning of communication, it has been estimated that 31,000 languages have existed.

828. The word "muggle" was added to the English dictionary and is defined as a person lacking a particular skill.

829. Noah Webster, the creator of the first ever American dictionary, learned twenty six languages so that he could understand and research the origins of his own country's tongue in order to write it.

830. The word "jay" used to be used as slang for a dull or stupid person, so when anyone ignored traffic regulations and crossed roads illegally, the person would be called a "jay walker."

831. Overmorrow is a word that means the day after tomorrow.

832. "Uncopyrightable" is the longest normal word you can use that doesn't contain repeat letters. "Subdermatoglyphic" is longer, however, it's only used by dermatologists.

833. "Sir, I demand, I am a maid named Iris" is the longest palindrome, that is, it makes the same sentence if you say it backwards.

834. The scientific word for picking your nose is rhinotillexomania. Rhino means nose, tillex means habitual picking, while mania means rage or fury.

835. Mandarin is the most spoken language in the world with 1.1 billion speakers.

836. The words Tokyo, Beijing, and Seoul all translate to "capital" in English.

837. The French-language Scrabble World Champion doesn't actually speak French. Nigel Richards memorized the whole French Scrabble dictionary, which contains 386,000 words, in nine weeks.

838. The term "googol" is actually a mathematical term for a very large number which is one followed by one hundred zeroes.

839. The word "checkmate" in chess comes from the Arabic "Shah Mat," which means the king is dead.

840. Vodka in Russian translates to "little water" in English.

841. Written language was invented by the Mayans, Egyptians, Chinese, and Sumerians independently.

842. Experts believe that New York is home to as many as 800 languages, making it the most linguistically-diverse city in the world.

843. Ioannis Ikonomou, the Chief Translator in the European Commission, can speak thirty two different languages. His native language is Greek, and he's the only in-house translator in the European Commission who's trusted to translate classified Chinese documents.

844. Just like all languages, sign language has different accents based on country, age, ethnicity, and whether the person is deaf or not.

845. There are approximately 6,500 languages spoken in the world today, however, 2,000 of those languages only have 1,000 speakers or less.

846. Grammatical Pedantry Syndrome is a form of OCD in which sufferers feel the need to correct every grammatical error they see.

847. The dot over the "j" or "i" is called a "tittle."

848. "I am" is the shortest English sentence.

Nature, Earth & The Universe

849. If you removed all the empty space from the atoms that make every human on Earth, all humans could fit into an apple.

850. The surface area in South America is greater than that of Pluto's.

851. The largest living creature on Earth is the Great Barrier Reef, which measures 1,200 miles (2,000 kilometers) long.

852. The Sun and the Moon appear to be the same size in our sky because of the amazing coincidence that the Moon is 400 times smaller, but also 400 times closer.

853. Graphene is pure carbon in the form of a very thin, nearly transparent sheet, only one atom thick, and it's the world's strongest material. It's one million times thinner than paper, but 200 times stronger than steel.

854. Earth is the only planet not named after a god.

855. There are more living organisms in a teaspoon of soil than there are humans in the world.

856. The largest volcano in our Solar System is also the largest mountain in the Solar System. It is Olympus Mons on Mars which is three times the height of Mt. Everest.

857. More than 20% of the world oxygen is produced in the Amazon rainforest.

858. Since Venus is not tilted on an axis like the Earth, it experiences no seasons.

859. The largest cave in the world is in Vietnam and it's called the "Son Doong Cave." It's just under six miles (nine kilometers) long, and its interior is so big that it has its own clouds

and forests. In fact, its ceiling is so high that you can fit an entire forty-story skyscraper inside.

860. There's a lake in Western Australia called "Lake Hillier" that has water that's naturally pink.

861. One-third of the Earth's surface is partially or total desert.

862. The oldest living system ever recorded is the cyanobacterias, a type of bacteria that originated 2.8 billion years ago.

863. The word "Sahara" in Arabic means desert, so "Desert Desert" in Arabic. It also once snowed in the Sahara back in 1979.

864. Fifty nine days on Earth is the equivalent of one on Mercury.

865. There is a hole in the ozone layer sitting right above Antarctica that is twice the size of Europe.

866. Saturn's largest moon named Titan has an atmosphere so thick and gravity so low that you can actually fly through it by flapping any sort of wings attached to your arms.

867. Around 350 to 420 million years ago, before trees were common, the Earth was covered in giant mushroom stalks.

868. The scent that lingers after it rains is called "petrichor."

869. It's estimated that the world's helium supply will run out within the next twenty to thirty years.

870. The Witwatsrand Basin was the densest area containing gold in the world. More than 40% of all the gold ever mined has come out of the Basin.

871. You would lose a third of your body weight on Mars due to lower gravity.

872. The biggest moon in our solar system is called "Ganymede" which is bigger than the planet Mercury.

873. Antarctica is considered a desert as it only receives two inches (fifty millimeters) of precipitation a year.

874. Astatine is the rarest element in the world with only thirty grams total in the Earth's crust.

875. Angel Falls is a waterfall in Venezuela that is the world's highest uninterrupted waterfall at a height of 3,200 feet (979 meters).

876. Portuguese navigator Ferdinand Magellan named the Pacific Ocean due to the calmness of the ocean. Pacific translates to peaceful.

877. Zenography is the study of the planet Jupiter.

878. Astronauts aboard the International Space Station see fifteen sunrises and fifteen sunsets a day averaging one every forty five minutes due to the station's proximity to the Earth and the speed of its orbit.

879. Over 50% of the oxygen supply we breathe comes from the Amazon rainforest.

880. The largest ocean on Earth is the Pacific Ocean covering 30% of the globe.

881. 90% of the Earth's ice is in Antarctica.

882. It rains diamonds on the planets Uranus and Neptune.

883. We know more about the surface of the Moon than we do about our own oceans.

884. The most polluted place on Earth is Lake Karachay, in Russia. It was used as a nuclear dumping site in the past by the Soviet Union. The radiation levels are so high that just one hour of exposure represents a lethal dose of radiation.

885. There's a phenomenon that occurs in the Mekong River in Thailand where red fireballs called "Naga Fireballs" randomly shoot into the air and nobody knows why it happens.

886. Only 30% of the Earth is covered by land.

887. The largest natural bridge in the world is the Ferry Bridge in China; it was virtually unknown to the rest of the world until it was observed on Google Maps.

888. Fire whirls, also known as fire tornadoes, are whirlwinds of flame that occur in countries where it's sufficiently hot enough such as Australia.

889. Scientists have discovered a planet using the Hubble telescope, a deep azure blue planet sixty three light years away that rains glass sideways.

890. If the Sun was scaled down to the size of a cell, the Milky Way would be the size of the United States.

891. Pluto is smaller than Russia.

892. Hudson Bar, in Canada, has less gravity than the rest of the Earth. It's unsure exactly why, but scientists hypothesize that it has something to do with the convection occurring in the Earth's mantle.

893. On the planet Venus it snows metal.

894. There are 100 to 400 billion stars in the Milky Way and more than 100 billion galaxies in the Universe.

895. Astronomers have found what appears to be one of the oldest known stars in the Universe which is located about 6,000 light-years away from Earth. The ancient star formed not long after the Big Bang, 13.8 billion years ago.

896. According to scientists, the weight of the average cloud is the same as 100 elephants.

897. The highest temperature ever recorded on Earth was in El Azizia on September 13, 1922, at 136 degrees Fahrenheit (fifty eight degrees Celsius).

898. The largest earthquake recorded was in Chile in 1960. It was placed at 9.4-9.6 on the magnitude scale and lasted for ten minutes.

899. The amount of water on Earth is constant, however, a billion years from now, the Sun will be 10% brighter, increasing the heat and causing the Earth to lose all its water.

900. The Challenger Deep in the Mariana Trench is the deepest point in Earth's oceans that we know about at 36,060 feet (10,994 meters).

901. Sand from the Sahara is blown by the wind all the way to the Amazon, recharging its minerals. The desert literally fertilizes the rainforest.

902. Over 99% of all species, equating to five billion species in total, that have ever been on Earth have died out.

903. Lightning strikes are not as rare as you think. Approximately 100 strikes hit the Earth per second. Each bolt can have up to a billion volts of electricity.

904. According to records, the last time that all the planets in the Solar System were aligned was 561 BC. The next alignment will take place in 2854.

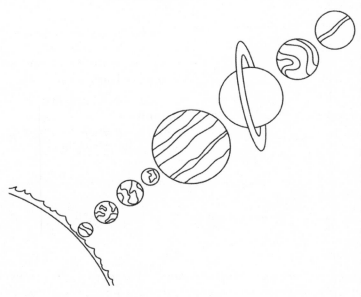

905. The Moon is capable of having "moonquakes." They are less frequent and intense as the ones on Earth however.

906. In 1977, we received a radio signal from space that lasted seventy two seconds and was dubbed "the wow signal." To this day we still don't know where it came from.

907. On Monday March 23, 2178, Pluto will complete its full orbit since its original discovery in 1930.

908. It takes 40,000 years for a photon of light to travel from the core of the Sun to its surface. For the same photon to travel from the Sun to Earth it only takes eight minutes.

909. Occasionally, in the arctic, the sun can appear square when it's on the horizon.

910. The Sahara is only in a dry period and is expected to be green again in 15,000 years.

911. Sunsets on Mars are blue.

Plants, Flowers & Trees

912. In Australia, there are trees that grow several different types of fruits known as fruit salad trees.

913. The average tree is made up of about 1% of living cells at any given time.

914. Bamboo can grow up to thirty five inches (ninety one centimeters) in a single day.

915. The Maldive coconut is the largest growing seed in the world.

916. In 2012, a Russian scientist regenerated an arctic flower known as "Silene stenophylla" that has been extinct for over 32,000 years from a seed that was buried by an ice-age squirrel.

917. The Eucalyptus deglupta, or more commonly known as the rainbow tree, is a tree that sheds its outer bark to reveal a bright green inner bark that turns blue, purple, orange, and maroon as it matures.

918. The average lifespan of a redwood tree is 500-700 years old while some coast redwoods have been known to live to over 2,000 years. They can grow to over 360 feet in height (109 meters).

919. There are more artificial Christmas trees sold in the world than real ones.

920. The world's biggest flower garden sits in the middle of a desert in Dubai, which has over 500,000 fresh flowers.

921. The country Brazil is named after a tree.

922. Only 15% of all plants are on land.

923. You can create 170 thousand pencils from the average tree.

924. There is a species of orchid that looks pretty much like a monkey. It only grows at high elevations, in certain mountainous areas of Ecuador, Colombia, and Peru.

925. The Baobab tree native to Madagascar can hold up to 31,000 gallons (120,000 liters) of water.

926. There is a flower called the "chocolate cosmos" that smells like chocolate but isn't edible.

927. There are roses that exist that are all black, but they can only be found in Halfeti, Turkey.

928. Sunflowers can be used to clean up radioactive waste. Their stems and leaves absorb and store pollutants. It's also why the sunflower is the international symbol for nuclear disarmament.

929. The largest organism in the known world today is a fungus that lives in the mountains of Oregon. It spans across 2.4 miles (3.8 kilometers).

930. The oldest recorded tree in the world is reported to be 9,550 years old located in Dalarna, Sweden.

931. In 2009, a new species of pitcher plant was found by scientists in the Philippines jungle, becoming the largest carnivorous plant ever discovered. It's called the Nepenthes attenboroughii, named after Sir David Attenborough. Carnivorous plants usually eat things like insects and spiders, but this one is so big that it actually eats rats.

932. Elephant grass can grow up to ten feet (three meters) tall that even elephants can hide in.

Really?

933. When Charles Darwin first discovered the huge tortoises on the Galapagos Islands, he tried to ride them.

934. In 2008, a businessman from Abu Dhabi spent $14.3 million at an auction to buy a license plate labeled "1," making it the world's most expensive license plate.

935. Yu Youhzen, a fifty three year old Chinese millionaire, works as a street cleaner for $228 per month to set a good example for her children.

936. In 2013, a man named Rogelio Andaverde was abducted from his home right in front of his wife by two masked men with guns. Luckily he returned two days later, unharmed. It was later discovered that he staged his own kidnapping just so he could go out and party with his friends.

937. A study by the University of Westminster in the UK determined that watching horror movies can burn up to almost 200 calories, the same as a half hour walk.

938. One of the iTunes user agreement policies explicitly states that you're not allowed to use the program to build nuclear, chemical, or biological weapons.

939. If you inhale a pea, it is possible to sprout and grow in your lungs.

940. The cheapest gas prices in the world belong to Venezuela at just over a penny a liter.

941. When you see an advertisement of a watch, it's almost always ten past ten.

942. Most of the dust you'll find in your house will be your dead skin.

943. The majority of lipsticks contain fish scales.

944. North Korea is the biggest counterfeiter of US currency.

945. In Russia, wealthy citizens often hire fake ambulances that beat the city traffic which are known as ambulance taxis. They can cost as much as $200/hour, have luxurious interiors, refreshments, and include caviar and champagne.

946. In 1985, a New Orleans man named Jerome Moody drowned at a party attended by 100 life guards who were celebrating having made it through the summer without a single drowning at a city pool.

947. The country of Niue, an island north of New Zealand, put various Pokémon on its one dollar coins in 2001. They included Pikachu, Squirtle, Meowth, Bulbasaur, and Charmander.

948. In the early years of the twentieth century, horses were causing so much pollution with their poop that automobiles were seen as the green alternative.

949. It was known that after examining the animals, Charles Darwin used to eat them too.

950. Walt Disney used to visit his parks in disguise and test ride operators to make sure that they weren't rushing guests.

951. All US presidents pay for their own food while staying at the White House.

952. The companies Audi, Bentley, Bugadi, Ducati, Lamborghini, and Porsche are all owned by Volkswagen.

953. At the University of Oaksterdam, you can graduate with a degree in Cannabis Cultivation.

954. There is currently 147 million ounces of gold in Fort Knox. At the price of about $1,776 per ounce, that's worth $261.6 billion.

955. More people die from attempting selfies than from shark attacks.

956. In 2012, a woman from New York named Deborah Stevens donated a kidney to her boss and was fired almost immediately after.

957. Jesse James, a notorious outlaw from the 1800's, once gave a widow who housed him enough money to pay off her debt collector, and then robbed the debt collector as the man left the widow's home.

958. Martin Luther King Jr. got a C in public speaking.

959. You're more likely to die on the way to buying a lottery ticket than you are to winning the lottery.

960. If you're taller than six foot two (two meters), you can't become an astronaut.

961. Both companies Louis Vuitton and Chanel burn their products at the end of the year preventing them to being sold at a discount.

962. A man named Sogen Kato was thought to be the oldest man in Tokyo until 2010 when officials arrived at his home to wish him a happy 111th birthday only to find his mummified remains. It turns out he had been dead for thirty years and his family had been collecting his pension money.

963. Falling in love produces the same high as taking cocaine.

964. At the end of the 1990's, BMW actually had to recall their GPS systems because male German drivers didn't want to take directions from a female driver.

965. On Good Friday in 1930, the BBC announced there was no news, followed by piano music.

966. In 2012, a sixty-three year old man named Wallace Weatherhold from Florida had his hand bitten off by an alligator and he was charged with illegally feeding the animal.

967. The average commuter wastes around forty two hours waiting in traffic each year.

968. The Romans considered women with unibrows attractive and desirable from 753 to 476 AD. Lots of women who didn't naturally have unibrows used paint to join their eyebrows to look prettier.

969. If you wear headphones for an hour, it will increase the amount of bacteria you have in your ear by 700 times.

970. Today there are more people suffering from obesity than there are suffering from hunger.

971. Despite having billions of dollars and being one of the wealthiest businessmen in the world, Ikea founder Ingvar Kamprad is notoriously cheap. He lives in a small home, eats at Ikea, takes the bus, and only flies economy class.

972. Bill Gates, Steve Jobs, Albert Einstein, Walt Disney, and Mark Zuckerberg all dropped out of school.

973. Benjamin Franklin wasn't trusted to write the US Declaration of Independence because it was feared he would conceal a joke in it.

974. President JFK purchased over a thousand Cuban cigars just hours before he ordered the Cuban trade embargo in 1962.

975. Carl Gugasian is serving seventeen years in jail after robbing fifty banks over a thirty year period, stealing $2 million.

976. A single factory in Ireland makes more than 90% of the world's botox.

977. Paul Getty was a billionaire who refused to pay the ransom of sixteen million dollars when his grandson was kidnapped. The group who kidnapped him later sent Paul the boy's severed ear and he finally accepted and said he'd pay three million dollars. He actually only gave a little over two million because that's all he could claim on tax.

978. In 2011, a ninety nine year old Italian named Antonio C. divorced his ninety six year old wife Rosa C. after finding secret love letters revealing that she had an affair in the 1940's.

979. Under extremely powerful pressure, peanut butter can be turned into diamonds.

980. In 2018, four billion people have access to the Internet yet 844 million people still don't have access to clean water.

981. In 1859, English settler Thomas Austin released twenty four rabbits onto his property in Australia; he thought that the introduction of a few rabbits could provide a touch of home in addition to a spot of hunting. By 1920, the rabbit population had reached ten billion.

982. On average, brunettes have less hairs on their head compared to red-haired and blondes.

983. Hitler was Time's "Man of the Year" in 1938.

984. Saddam Hussein, the late President of Iraq, wrote several novels and a number of poems which were published anonymously.

985. In 2017, 19% of brides said they met their spouse online. This industry now brings in $3 billion a year.

986. In order to be a London Black Cab driver, one is expected to know 25,000 roads and 50,000 points of interest to pass the test called "The Knowledge." Applicants usually need twelve appearances and thirty four months of preparation to pass it.

987. Deceased North Korean leader Kim Jong II's official biography lists among his achievements a thirty eight-shot round of golf, the ability to control weather, the need to never have to poop, and being the creator of the hamburger.

988. It costs 1.5 cents to make a penny and the US Mint issued $46 million worth of these coins in 2018.

989. In China, the extremely wealthy can avoid prison terms by hiring body doubles.

990. Before toilet paper was invented, Americans used to use corn cobs.

Royalty

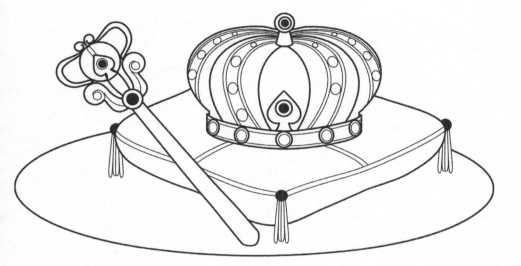

991. Queen Elizabeth the second has someone to wear the shoes she gets before she wears them to make sure they're comfortable.

992. The Queen of England legally owns one third of the Earth's surface.

993. In the United Kingdom, the queen cannot be arrested no matter what crime she commits. This is because the Crown itself is the prosecuting force in the UK and hence the Crown cannot verse the Crown itself. The other members of the Royal Family do not share the same immunity.

994. Bhumibol Adulyadej, the King of Thailand, was actually born in Cambridge, Massachusetts, in the United States, in 1927. When he was born, the hospital room that he was delivered in was briefly declared Thai territory so he could be born on Thai soil.

995. A prince in Abu Dhabi spent $2.5 million to create a Mercedes Benz with a V10 engine with 1,600 horsepower that goes 0 to 100 in less than two seconds running on biofuel.

996. Queen Elizabeth does not have a passport. Since the British passport is issued in her name, she does not need to possess one, however, the other members of the Royal Family do.

997. Royal tradition states that Prince Charles and Prince William cannot board the same plane together in case there is a crash and the monarch loses two heirs at once. Technically the same rule applies for Prince William and his five-year-old son, Prince George.

Science

998. Sound can travel quicker through solids. This is because molecules in a solid medium are much closer together than those in a liquid or gas, allowing sound waves to travel more quickly through it.

999. It is false that you can bite through a finger as easily as a carrot. It takes 200 newtons to bite through a raw carrot and 1,485 newtons just to cause a fracture to a finger.

1000. A solid glass ball can bounce higher than a rubber ball when dropped from the same height. A solid steel ball can bounce even higher than a solid glass ball.

1001. Hot water freezes quicker than cold water. This is called the "Mpemba effect," named after a Tanzanian student who discovered it.

1002. Light doesn't actually move at the speed of light. The full quote is actually: "the speed of light in a vacuum" which is 186,282 miles (299,792 kilometers) per second. If you were able to move at this speed, you could go around Earth seven and a half times in a second.

1003. You would weigh more at the poles than you would weigh at the equator, however, the difference would only be 0.5% approximately. You would weigh slightly more at sea level than at the top of a mountain. This is due to oblateness and gravitational pull.

1004. Aerogel, also known as frozen smoke, is one of the world's lowest density solids being made up of anywhere from 95-99% air. It's almost impossible to see or feel, but it can support 4,000 times its own weight.

1005. The first man made element was technetium created in 1937. It is used for medical diagnostic studies and as a corrosion inhibitor for steel.

1006.   The scientific term for pins and needles is paresthesia.

1007.   Only 0.1% of an atom is matter. The rest is air.

1008.   If you put an apple in the sea, it will float because it's less dense than seawater.

1009.   Sterling silver is not completely made out of silver. A little copper is added as pure silver is too soft and would bend otherwise.

1010.   In 1951, a woman named Henrietta Lacks died of cervical cancer, but her tumor cells were removed and later discovered to be the first ever human cells that could thrive in a lab. Her cells have been the subject of more than 74,000 studies, many of which have yielded profound insights into cell biology, cancer, vaccine, and cloning.

1011.   LSD has been known to cure Post Traumatic Stress Disorder, such as in the case of Yehiel De-Nur, a Holocaust survivor who, after taking the drug, was able to sleep for the first time in thirty years without nightmares.

1012.   Two neuroscientists were successful in implanting a fake memory in a mouse's brain in 2012. The mouse was aghast as it remembered something that never really happened to it.

1013.   A flame is round and blue when in zero gravity.

1014.   Scientists from Georgia State University have found that monkeys are susceptible to optical illusions, just like humans. To test this, capuchin and rhesus monkeys looked at a visual illusion where two dots were surrounded by rings, but were actually the same size, and they were tricked much like many people were.

Shocking

1015.   In 2011, a forty six year old man named Mark Bradford hunted down and choked a thirteen year old boy who killed him several times in the game "Call of Duty."

1016.   In 1967, the Prime Minister of Australia went missing. It was only four decades after he went missing that it was confirmed that he had accidentally drowned.

1017.   In 1971, a man named Jean-Claude Romand lied about passing important medical exams and he continued crafting elaborate lies until everyone he knew thought he was an actual medical doctor. He got away for it for eighteen years until he eventually killed his entire family to avoid being revealed.

1018.   Doctors with messy handwriting kill more than 7,000 people and injure over a million people each year due to receiving the wrong medication.

1019.   In 1954, a man named John Thomas Doyle committed suicide by jumping off the Golden Gate Bridge. His suicide note read absolutely no reason other than "I have a toothache."

1020.   The first recorded human flight with artificial wings in history was in the 6th century in China. Emperor Kao Yang would strap prisoners to kites and throw them off a building to see if they could fly.

1021.   The longest someone has been in a coma and come out of it is thirty seven years. A six year old went to the hospital for a routine appendectomy, went under general anesthesia, and didn't come out for reasons doctors can't explain.

1022.   In 1567, Hans Steininger, who once had the longest beard in the world at 4.5 feet (1.4 meters) long, died when he broke his neck after accidentally stepping on it.

1023.   Luis Garavito, one of the world's most dangerous serial killers with 140 victims, had his sentence reduced to only twenty two years and could be out as early as 2021.

1024.   In 2006, an extremely old clam was found by a group of researchers in Iceland. In order to find out its age, researchers didn't count the rings on the outside of the clam, but instead they opened it and counted the rings on the inside, causing the clam to die. The clam turned out to be 507 years old, the world's oldest animal.

1025.   Lake Chagan is the only lake artificially created by a nuclear test. Even though the nuclear test was fired in 1965, it's still unsafe for swimming due to radiation.

1026.   In 2008, a Japanese man noticed that food in his home was disappearing so he set up a webcam and discovered that a fifty eight year old homeless woman was living in his closet for an entire year.

1027.   Ramon Artagaveytia once survived a sinking ship in 1871. He was so scared from this experience he didn't get on another ship till forty one years later. Unfortunately for him that ship was Titanic.

1028.   In 2011, a New Zealand trucker named Steven McCormack fell on a high-pressure valve which lodged in his butt and inflated him to twice his size nearly killing him. He did survive, but it took a full three days to burp and fart out the excess air.

1029.   Vending machines kill about thirteen people a year.

1030.   The biggest family in the world is from Baktawng, India, where father Ziona Chana has ninety four children by thirty nine different wives.

1031.   The pollution in China is so bad in some parts that just being in that area for one day is the equivalent of smoking twenty one cigarettes.

1032.   Some Japanese companies such as Sony, Toshiba, and Panasonic have banishment rooms where they transfer surplus employees and give them useless tasks or even nothing to do until they become disheartened or depressed enough to quit on their own, thus avoiding paying them full benefits.

1033.   In 1886, a man named H.H. Holmes built a three-story hotel in Chicago specifically to kill people in it. Its design included stairways to nowhere and a maze of over 100 windowless rooms which he used to kill over 200 people.

1034.   There has only been 240 years of peace in the last 3,000 years.

1035.   An Indonesian boy named Aldi Rizal began chain smoking when he was just eighteen months old and continued smoking over forty cigarettes a day until he was five years old when he was sent to rehab.

1036.   The strongest beer in the world is called "Snake Venom" containing 67.5% alcohol.

1037.   It is estimated that malaria has been responsible for half of the deaths of everyone who has ever lived.

1038.   The world record for the most bones broken in a lifetime is held by Evel Knievel, the pioneer of motorcycle long jumping exhibitions, who has suffered 433 fractured bones.

1039.   Approximately one in every six Jewish people killed in the Holocaust died at Auschwitz.

1040.   Sharks kill about twelve people a year. People kill about eleven thousand sharks an hour.

1041.   Four American presidents have been killed by gunshot.

1042.   In 1967, a magazine called "Berkeley Barb" published a fake story about extracting hallucinogenic chemical from bananas to raise moral questions about banning drugs. Unfortunately people didn't realize it was a hoax and began smoking banana peels to try to get high.

1043.   You are 14% more likely to die on your birthday than any other day.

1044.   In Bern, Switzerland, there's a 500 year old statue of a man eating a sack of babies and nobody is sure why.

1045.   The "China National Highway 110" traffic jam was considered the longest traffic jam in history. It was sixty two miles (100 kilometers) long and lasted eleven days.

1046.   The brothers Adolf Dassler and Rudolf Dassler, who started Puma and Adidas, were part of the Nazi party.

1047.   The youngest mother in medical history was Lina Medina from Peru who gave birth when she was five.

1048.   Your mobile phone carries ten times more bacteria than your toilet seat.

1049.   As of 2016, about 280 climbers have died on Everest. Their bodies are so well preserved that they are used as markers.

Sports

1050.   The temperature of tennis balls affects how a ball can bounce. Wimbledon go through over fifty thousand tennis balls a year that are kept at sixty eight degrees Fahrenheit (twenty degrees Celsius) to make sure only the best are used.

1051.   In 2022, the World Cup will be played in Lusail, Qatar, a city that doesn't even exist yet.

1052.   The longest human jump is further than the longest horse jump. In the 1968 Olympics, the world record was set at 8.9 meters while the record for a horse is twenty eight feet (8.4 meters).

1053.   Jousting is the official sport in the state of Maryland.

1054.   Today's gold medals are only 1.3% gold. The last time a pure gold medal was given out was in the 1912 Stockholm Olympics.

1055.   A tribe in West Africa, known as "The Matami Tribe," play a version of football which consists of using a human skull as the ball.

1056.   In 2013, Sean Conway became the first man ever to swim the entire length of Great Britain. The 900 miles (1,400 kilometers) trek took him 135 days to complete. Ninety were spent in water while the rest were spent avoiding bad weather and resting.

1057.   There is a real sport called "Banzai Skydiving" which involves throwing your parachute out of the plane and then jumping out after it.

1058.   Quebec only finished paying off its 1976 Summer Olympics debt thirty years later, in 2006.

1059.   The most popular sport in the world is football. Second place goes to cricket followed by field hockey.

1060.   As a child, Muhammad Ali was refused an autograph from his boxing idol Sugar Ray Robinson. When Ali became a prized fighter, he vowed to never deny an autograph request, which he honored throughout his entire career.

1061.   In 1984, when the Air Jordans were introduced, they were banned by the NBA. Michael Jordan wore them anyways as Nike was willing to pay the $5,000 fine each time he stepped onto the court.

1062.   In 1947, Sugar Ray Robinson, one of the greatest boxers of all time, backed out of a fight because he had a dream that he was going to kill his opponent. After being convinced to fight, he went into the ring and actually killed his opponent.

1063.   The highest scoring soccer game in history recognized by the Guinness Book of World Records was 149 to zero between two teams in Madagascar in 2002. It happened because one of the teams began scoring on themselves in protest of a bad call by one of the referees.

1064.   There's a sport called "squirrel fishing," in which participants try to catch squirrels and lift them into the air by using a nut on a fishing pole.

1065.   Wales holds a world mountain bike bog snorkeling championship. Contenders have to ride a mountain bike as fast as they can along the bottom of a bog, which has a 6.5 feet (two meter) deep, water-filled trench. To make it more difficult, the bikes that they use have led-filled frames, the tires are filled with water, and the competitors wear led weight belts so that they don't float off of their bikes.

Technology, Internet & Videogames

1066.   Workers of Amazon's distribution centers can be expected to walk up to eleven miles (seventeen kilometers) per shift picking up an order once every thirty three seconds.

1067.   When they made "Breakout" for Atari, Steve Jobs and Steve Wozniak agreed to split the pay 50/50. Atari gave Jobs $5,000 for it, but Jobs only told Wozniak he got $700, only giving him $350.

1068.   Intel employs a futuris named Brian David Johnson whose job is to determine what life would be like to live ten to fifteen years in the future.

1069.   Yang Yuanquing, Lenovo's CEO, received a $3 million bonus as a reward due to record profits in 2012, which he redistributed to 10,000 of Lenovo's employees. He did the exact same thing in 2013.

1070.   Shigeru Miyamoto, the creator of the famous games Mario, Zelda, and Donkey Kong, was banned from riding a bicycle. This is because he became so valuable to Nintendo that they didn't want to risk anything happening to him, forcing him to drive a car instead.

1071.   A hacker group named UGNazi once took down Papa John's website because the company was two hours later than expected in delivering their food.

1072.   There are at least seven apps on the app store that are priced $999.99, which is the maximum price you can charge on the app store.

1073.   If a Google employee dies, their spouse gets half their salary for the next ten years, stock benefits, and their children get $1,000/month until they're nineteen.

1074.   Facebook tracks and records your IP address as well as the URL of every website that you visit that uses any of its social plugins such as the like button.

1075.   There are fewer than fifty of the original Apple 1 computers in existence with some of them selling for over $50,000.

1076.   In 1998, Larry Page and Sergey Brin, the founders of Google, offered to sell their little startup to AltaVista for $1 million so they could resume their studies at Stanford. They were rejected, and have now grown the empire to $101 billion as of 2019.

1077.   There was a third Apple founder named Ronald Wayne who once owned 10% of the whole company. He decided to sell that 10% stake for $800 in 1976.

1078.   In 2009, Wikipedia permanently banned the church of Scientology from editing any articles.

1079.   The one click option was invented by Amazon, who have a patent on it, and Apple pays them a licensing fee to use it.

1080.   In 2013, over 200 strangers responded to a Facebook invitation to attend a funeral for British veteran James McConnel, who had no friends or family members to attend otherwise.

1081.   Nomophobia is the fear of being without mobile phone coverage.

1082.   Michael Birch, the founder of the social networking site Bebo, sold it to AOL for $850 million in 2008, only to later buy it back for a million dollars in 2013.

1083.   Futureme.org is a website where you can send e-letters to yourself at any time in the future.

1084.   Jeff Bezos net worth is so high that it wouldn't be worth him picking up a $100 bill if he dropped it. In fact, he has to spend $28 million a day just to stop getting richer.

1085.   The average iPhone only costs $200 to make.

1086.   Watson, IBM's artificially intelligent computer, learned how to swear from the urban dictionary. Because of that, it began talking sassy so scientists had to remove the entire urban dictionary database from its memory.

1087.   Internet addiction disorder, also known as "IAD," is a real mental disorder in which somebody engages in addictive, compulsive, or pathological Internet use.

1088.   There are over four million apps available for download on both the Android and Apple app store.

1089.   300 hours of video are uploaded to YouTube every minute and almost five billion videos are watched on YouTube every single day.

1090.   Amazon is the first company to ever hit a trillion dollars.

1091.   The first web page went live on August 6, 1991, and was dedicated to information.

1092.   Over 90% of mobile phone sales in Japan are for waterproof devices because the Japanese are so fond of their mobile phones they even use them in the shower.

1093.   Google, Amazon, Microsoft, and Facebook alone have 1.2 million terabytes of information stored on the Internet.

1094.   If you Google "Zerg rush," Google will begin to eat the search page.

1095.   The first email was sent in 1971. The email was sent to the computer right next to it as a test.

1096.   Theringfinders.com is an online site where you can find metal-detecting experts you can hire for a fixed fee to search for and find items of jewelry that you may have lost. They've successfully recovered 3,000 items worth over $5.2 million.

1097.   1,000 selfies are posted to Instagram every ten seconds. This is ninety three million selfies a day.

1098.   97% of all emails sent are spam.

1099.   Digital storage doesn't go up in measurements of thousands. 1024 bits make a byte, 1024 bytes makes up a kilobyte followed by megabyte, gigabyte, terabyte, and petabyte.

1100.   In April of 2014, the Danish government built an exact replica of their country in the online game Minecraft using four trillion Minecraft building blocks. It was intended for educational purposes, but within weeks, American players had invaded the game planting American flags everywhere and blowing things up.

1101.   Half the world has never made or received a phone call.

1102.   The red mushrooms featured in Nintendo's Mario games are based on a real species of a fungi called "Amanita muscaria." They're known for their hallucinogenic properties and can distort the size of perceived objects. This is also the same mushroom that is referenced in Alice in Wonderland.

1103.   A software company called "PC Pitstop" once hid a $1,000 prize in their terms of service just to see if anyone would read it. After five months and three thousand sales later, someone finally did.

1104.   The four ghosts in Pacman are all programmed to do certain things. Blinky, the red ghost, chases you; Pinky, the pink ghost, simply tries to position herself in front of Pacman; Inky, the blue ghost, tries to position himself in the same way; and Clyve, the orange ghost, moves randomly.

1105.   The UN has deemed access to the Internet a human right.

1106.   The famous torrent site Pirate Bay once tried to buy its own island to make their own country with no copyright laws.

1107.   The app Candy Crush was making $956,000 a day in its prime.

1108.   There are 2.32 billion monthly active users on Facebook as of 31st December, 2018.

1109.   There are approximately 250,000 active patents applicable to the smartphone.

1110.   In a study conducted by the Bay State Medical Center in Springfield, approximately 68% of people experience phantom vibrations syndrome, a sensory hallucination where you mistakenly think your phone is buzzing in your pocket.

1111.   Jeff Bezos, the owner of Amazon.com, is also the owner of the Washington Post.

1112.   Google rents goats to replace lawn mowers at their Mountain View headquarters.

1113.   Zoe Pemberton, a ten year old girl from the UK, attempted to sell her grandma on eBay because she found her annoying and wanted her to disappear.

1114.   It took approximately seventy five years for the telephone to reach fifty million users, the radio thirty eight years, thirteen years for the television, four for the Internet, two for Facebook, and only nineteen days for Pokémon Go.

1115.   There are currently 1.6 billion live websites on the web right now. However, 99% of these sites you cannot access through Google and it's known as the Deep Web.

1116.   In the year 2020, there will be approximately forty billion gadgets connected to the Internet.

1117.   Google actually hires camels to carry its trekker camera in order to get street views of deserts.

War & Military World

1118. Russia trained and deployed 40,000 anti-tank dogs in World War Two. The dogs were loaded with explosives and trained to run under tanks where they would be detonated, except many of the dogs became scared and ran back to their owner's trenches where they killed their own people.

1119. There were at least forty two known assassination plots against Hitler.

1120. Chiune Sugihara was a famous Japanese diplomat that operated in Lithuania during World War Two. He helped more than 6,000 Jewish refugees escape to Japanese territory by issuing them transit visas risking his life and his family's life in the process.

1121. In World War Two, Jacklyn Lucas lied his way into the military and became the youngest marine ever to earn a medal of honor. When he was seventeen, he threw himself on two live grenades to protect his squad members and survived.

1122. 144 successful prisoners escaped Auschwitz.

1123. There are now twenty two countries worldwide that have no army, navy, or air force.

1124. During the Cold War, the US's passcode to nuclear missiles was eight zeroes so they could fire them as quick as possible.

1125. Hitler planned on invading Switzerland but gave in as it was too difficult with the surrounding mountains.

1126. Russia and Japan have still not signed a peace treaty to end World War Two.

1127. During World War Two, prisoners in Canadian war camps were so well treated that they were given games and entertainment like soccer tournaments and musical groups. When the war ended, many of them didn't want to leave Canada.

1128.   There was a bear named Wojtek that fought in the Polish army during World War II. His name meant "he who enjoys war." He carried shells to the front line and was taught to salute; he became a mascot for the soldiers and even developed a habit for drinking beer and smoking cigarettes. He survived the war and lived the rest of his life in the Edinburgh Zoo.

1129. In 1945, a man named Tsutomu Yamaguchi survived the atomic blast at Hiroshima only to catch the morning train so that he could arrive at his job on time in Nagasaki where he survived another atomic blast.

1130. Since 1945, all British tanks have come equipped with tea making facilities.

1131. The most successful interrogator of World War Two was Hanns Scharff who, instead of using torture, would befriend the prisoner. He would gain their trust by taking them to a cinema on camp and sharing a coffee or tea with them.

1132.   Being clean-shaven became popular in the US after the troops returned home as heroes from World War I. Soldiers had been required to shave so that gas masks could securely fit on their face.

1133.   The British submarine HMS Trident had a fully grown reindeer onboard as a pet for six weeks during WWII.

1134.   Before Nazis used the salute we now know as Hitler's salute, it was called the "Bellamy salute," and it was used by Americans to salute the flag until it was replaced in 1942 by the hand over heart salute.

1135.   Every year the Netherlands sends 20,000 tulip bulbs to Canada to thank them for their help in the Second World War.

1136.   During World War Two, two Japanese officers named Tokiashi Mukai and Tsuyoshi Noda had a contest or race to

see who could kill 100 people first using only a sword. Disturbingly, it was covered like a sporting event in Japanese newspapers with regular updates on the score.

1137.   The Filipino flag is flown with its red stripe up in times of war and blue side up in times of peace.

1138.   The US Navy owns over thirty killer dolphins. They are trained to hunt, and carry guns with toxic darts in them that are lethal enough to kill someone in one shot.

1139.   Chinese soldiers stick needles in their shirt collars in order to keep a straight posture during military parades.

1140.   Hitler collected Jewish artifacts for a museum of what he hoped to be an extinct race after the Second World War.

1141.   Ambrose Burnside was a general in the American Civil War known for his unusual facial hairstyle, and is where the term "sideburns" come from.

1142.   The largest detonated bomb in the world was the Tsar Bomb on October 30, 1961, by the Soviet Union. The blast was 3,000 times stronger than the bomb used on Hiroshima. The impact was strong enough to break windows 560 miles (900 kilometer) away.

1143.   The wars between Romans and Persians lasted about 721 years, the longest conflict in human history.

1144.   David B. Leak was an American soldier from the Korean War who was given the Medal of Honor after killing five soldiers, four with his bare hands, while giving medical attention to one of his comrades after being shot.

If you enjoyed this book and learned anything, it would mean the world to me if you could please leave a review so others can easily find this book and itch their curiosity!

Did you enjoy the book or learn something new? It really helps out small publishers like Scott Matthews if you could leave a quick review on Amazon so others in the community can also find the book! You can scan the QR code below which will take you straight to the review page!

Made in the USA
Las Vegas, NV
27 November 2021

35224814R00059